SHIPWRECKS

SHIPW

RECKS

Karen Farrington

THUNDER BAY
P·R·E·S·S

This edition published in 1999 by
Thunder Bay Press
5880 Oberlin Drive, Suite 400
San Diego, California 92121
1-800-284-3580

http://www.admsweb.com

Produced by
PRC Publishing Ltd,
Kiln House, 210 New Kings Road, London SW6 4NZ

ISBN 1 57145 159 5
(or Library of Congress CIP data if available)

1 2 3 4 5 98 99 00 01 02

Printed and bound in China

Acknowledgements

The publisher wishes to thank the following agencies and
photographers for supplying the illlustrations in this book:

Pages 2-3, 23 (both) and 26 courtesy of Pictor International;
Pages 6-7 courtesy of Corbis/Greg Bos; page 9 (top)
courtesy of Corbis/Historical Picture Archive;
page 9 (bottom) courtesy of Corbis/Philadelphia Museum of
Art; pages 8, 13 (bottom), 94 (top), 105 (bottom) courtesy
of Corbis/Bettmann; page 16 (bottom) courtesy of
Corbis/Jonathan Blair, page 18 (top, inset) courtesy of
Corbis/The Mariner's Museum, page 37 (top) courtesy of
Jeffrey L Rotman, page 47 (top) courtesy of Bettmann/UPI,
page 58 (top), courtesy of Corbis/Layne Kennedy,
page 77 (bottom) courtesy of Corbis/Lowell Georgia, page
86 (bottom) courtesy of Corbis, page 101 (inset) courtesy of
The Hulton-Deutsch Collection/Corbis; page 105 (top)
courtesy of Corbis/The Mariners' Museum;
Pages 10, 12, 14 (bottom), 16 (top left, right), 20-21,
25 (both), 27, 28-29, 33 (all), 37 (bottom), 39 (both),
43 (both), 44 (both), 48 (middle, bottom), 51 (top), 53,
55 (both), 60 (all), 73 (middle), 77 (top), 79 (both), 80 (all),
83 (all), 85 (both), 86 (top), 94 (bottom), 95 (top),
96 (bottom), 99 (both), 100-101 (main), 105 (middle),
110 (both), 113 (top), 113 (both), 114, 115 (both), 116-117,
118 (bottom), 120 (both), 123 (top), 124 (both), 125 (both),
128-129 (main and inset, bottom left) and 134 (bottom)
courtesy of The Hulton Getty Picture Collection;
Page 11 courtesy of The Image Bank; page 14 (top)
courtesy of Archive Photos; page 134 (top) courtesy of
Reuters/Mike Blake/Archive Photos;
Pages 18-19 (main), 66 (top), 91 (bottom), 93 (bottom),
95 (bottom), 118 (top) and back cover picture courtesy of
David Williams;
Page 19 (top, inset) courtesy of the National Oceanic and
Atmospheric Administration Office of NOAA Corps
Operations/Department of Commerce, USA;
Pages 31 (both), 48 (top), 58 (bottom), 93 (top), 96 (top),
103 (both), 108 (middle, bottom), 113 (bottom),
116-117 (main), 123 (bottom), 126 (both), 129 (inset,
bottom right), 131 (both), 133 (both), 137 (all),
139 (bottom), and 142 (both) courtesy of the Bison Picture
Library;
Page 47 (bottom) courtesy of the Peabody Essex Museum,
Salem, Massachusetts;
Pages 51 (bottom), 57, 68-69 and front cover picture
courtesy of Frank Gibson of Penzance;
Pages 62-63 (main and inset), 66 (bottom), 91 (top) and
108 (top) courtesy of the Peninsular & Oriental Navigation
Company;
Page 73 (bottom) courtesy of Harland & Wolff;
Page 73 (top) courtesy of Titanic Heritage;
Page 75 (top) courtesy of The Illustrated London News;
Page 75 (middle) courtesy of the Public Record Office;
Page 75 (bottom) courtesy of Low Films International;
Page 139 (top and middle) courtesy of Kari Lehtinen;
Page 143 (top) courtesy of the Austin J Brown Picture
Library.

CONTENTS

Introduction   6

Shipwrecks   28
Kyrenia ship—288 B.C.   30
Kinneret boat—1st century A.D.   30
The White Ship—November 25, 1120   30
Mary Rose—1545   32
Spanish Armada—1588   32
Nuestra Senora de Atocha—September 4, 1622   34
Blessing of Burntisland—July 10, 1633   35
Nuestra Senora de las Maravillas—January 4, 1656   35
French Fleet—May 11, 1678   36
H.M.S. *Association*—October 22, 1707   38
English Armada—1711   38
Diana—March 5 1817   40
Essex—November 20, 1820   40
Washington—May 14, 1831   41
Caledonia—1842   41
Lady Elgin—September 8, 1851   42
Birkenhead—1852   42
Pennsylvania—1858   42
U.S.S. *Monitor*—December 29, 1862   45
Sultana—April 27, 1865   45
Atlantic—April 1, 1873   46
Princess Alice—September 1878   46
Sunrise—June 19, 1882   49
Lucerne—November 17, 1886   49
H.M.S. *Serpent*—November 10, 1890   50
H.M.S. *Victoria*/H.M.S. *Camperdown*—June 22, 1893   50
Aden—June 9, 1897   52
U.S.S. *Maine*—February 15, 1898   52
La Bourgogne—July 4, 1898   54
Mohegan—October 13, 1898   56
Stella—March 30, 1899   56
Cuvier—March 9, 1900   56
Saale—June 30, 1900   56
Fedora—September 20, 1901   59
City of Rio de Janeiro—February 22, 1902   59
Camorta—April 1902   59
General Slocum—June 15, 1904   61
Norge—June 28, 1904   61
Australia—June 29, 1904   61
Sirio—August 4, 1906   64
Prinzessin Victoria Luise—December 16, 1906   64
Dakota—March 7, 1907   65
Neustria—November 1908   65
Republic—January 23, 1909   65
Slavonia—June 10, 1909   67
Waratah—July 1909   67
Lucania—August 14, 1909   68
Orinoco—August 18, 1909   68

La Seyne—November 14, 1909   70
General Chanzy—February 10, 1910   70
Madalene Cooney—December 28, 1911   70
Patrician—March 15, 1912   70
Titanic—April 14, 1912   71
Volturno—October 1913   76
Edmund Fitzgerald—November 9, 1913   76
Empress of Ireland—May 29, 1914   78
Montrose—December 1914   78
Lusitania—May 7, 1915   81
Eastland—July 24, 1915   84
Marowijne—August 1915   84
Ancona—November 8, 1915   87
Mont Blanc—December 30, 1917   87
City of Athens—May 1, 1918   88
Afrique—January 13, 1920   88
Hong Koh—March 18, 1921   89
Egypt—May 20, 1922   90
Principessa Mafalda—October 25, 1927   90
Vestris—November 12, 1928   90
Celtic—December 10, 1928   92
Dresden—June 20, 1934   92
Morro Castle—September 8, 1934   92
Ausonia—October 18, 1935   97
Lafayette—May 4, 1938   97
Athenia—September 3, 1939   97
Politician—1941   98
Grand Camp—April 16, 1947   98
Princess Victoria—January 31, 1953   102
Andrea Doria—July 25, 1956   102
Hans Hedtoft—January 30, 1959   106
Dara—April 9, 1961   107
Save—July 8, 1961   109
Venezuela—March 17, 1962   109
Yarmouth Castle—November 13, 1965   111
Heraklion—December 12, 1966   111
Torrey Canyon—March 1967   112
Wahine—April 11, 1968   117
Seawise University—January 9, 1972   119
Amoco Cadiz—March 16, 1977   122
Derbyshire—September 10, 1980   127
Herald of Free Enterprise—March 6, 1987   130
Cason—December 5, 1987   132
Exxon Valdez—March 1989   135
Marchioness—August 20, 1989   136
Neptune—February 17, 1993   138
Estonia—September 29, 1994   138
Achille Lauro—November 30, 1994   141
Sea Empress—February 15, 1996   143

Index   144

INTRODUCTION

The rarest coal on Earth sells for ten dollars a chunk. It comes complete with its own protective sack and a signed Certificate of Origin. Each precious piece has been individually weighed, inventoried, and meticulously recorded by U.S. Customs. If you want, you can even burn it!

Nobody does. Thousands of similar bits of coal have been scooped up from the debris-strewn seabed around the *Titanic*, 13,000 ft. (4,000 m.) beneath the surface of the North Atlantic, to adorn mantelpieces the world over. They were the first items salvaged from the ship to go on general sale, although more than 4,000 other artifacts ranging from porcelain plates to bottles of beer have been recovered for exhibition.

Some people argue that selling "ornamental" coal from a shipwreck that cost more than 1,500 lives is disturbing, not to say downright offensive. (The *Titanic* is, after all, the official grave of those who died.) However, this global obsession with a doomed liner is far more complex. The 20th century is littered with disasters, many involving much greater loss of life, yet international marketing companies show no sign of queuing up to sell shattered bricks from earthquake zones or hurricane-damaged roof tiles.

The fact is that, in occupying seven-tenths of the Earth's surface, the sea holds a fascination for us all. Shipwrecks conjure up images of drama, adventure, romance, terror, and survival. Above all, they are symbols of their age, microcosms of the societies that created them.

No wonder technological advances are signaling boomtime for marine archeology. Tremendous leaps forward in microchip expertise that allow heretofore unprecedented exploration opportunities have changed the public perception of shipwrecks. For years they were considered flash points of drama, which all too frequently turned into underwater graves. The recovery of long-lost ships and their cargoes wasn't even on the agenda. That is no longer the case. There are increasingly few wrecks that cannot be explored and examined by divers.

PREVIOUS PAGE: The stricken Scandinavian Star, April 8, 1990. The ferry caught fire off the coast of Sweden—the death toll amounted to nearly 150 passangers.

LEFT: A reward poster at a marina for the yacht *Saba Bank*, which went missing in the Bermuda Triangle on March 10, 1974. This legendary and mysterious area has also been called the Devil's Triangle due to the unexplained losses of both ships and aircraft which have occured in the region.

RIGHT: *The miracle of Saint Nicholas of Tolentino.* In times past it was considered lucky to have a holy man on board a vessel. This picture from c. 1456 shows the saint quelling the elements by the power of prayer. Before weather systems were understood it was common that storms would be attributed to a variety of supernatural sources.

BELOW: A divinely ordained storm was sent to punish Jonah for disobeying God's will. He was cast overboard, swallowed by a whale, and lived in its stomach for three days and nights. Jonah was then vomited up onto shore and was quick to return to God's work!

LEFT: Ringing the Lutine Bell, April 8, 1939. An employee sounding the bell of the frigate *Lutine* (lost off the Dutch coast in 1799) which hangs in the Underwriters' Room at Lloyd's of London, headquarters of marine insurance. The bell is traditionally struck each time news of a loss at sea is received.

The subtle history of marine archeology begins with a Greek sponge diver called Elias Stadiatos. In October 1900 he was part of a crew diving off Pinakakia, on the rugged north coast of the island of Antikythera.

Divers had worked the Aegean for centuries, training themselves to submerge below 200 ft. (60 m.). with only a single breath of air, a stone sinker, a glass minute-timer, and a safety line. By Stadiatos's day, things had advanced to the point where divers took turns using a copper helmet and canvas wet suit. Even so, it was a dangerous business. Many young men suffered agonies from the "bends"—decompression sickness caused by the blood's absorption of nitrogen gas—and fatalities were high.

That October morning, Stadiatos was the first diver over the side, resurfacing some five minutes later. From his panicky actions crew members realized that something was wrong and quickly twisted off his helmet. Instantly, the jabbering man poured out details of his nightmare dive, a dive in which he had seen "a heap of dead, naked women and rotting green corpses." Minutes later his captain, Dimitrios Kondos, was swimming down

RIGHT: Prince William Sound, southeastern Alaska. The northwestern coast of North America is plagued by severe weather conditions, including ice, fog, and storms. These have overwhemed many fine vessels over the years and mariners remain wary of the area. Even when a ship is equipped with the most up to date technology and the crew are experienced and alert, the region is highly perilous.

to discover the truth. He returned with a badly corroded bronze arm attached to his lifeline—part of an ancient statue that had lain on the seabed among dozens of bronze and marble sculptures that had been carried in the hold of a wrecked Roman argosy. The age of the marine treasure hunter had begun and the Antikythera find sparked off a huge operation financed by the Greek government.

As diving and underwater search equipment became more sophisticated—refined by the scientific advances of two world wars—a tantalizing picture began to emerge of shipwrecks around the world. There was obvious appeal to archeologists, for whom wrecks were priceless time capsules of their age. But entrepreneurs and financiers were equally beguiled. The seabed offered a chance to make careers and secure fortunes.

The result is that modern-day shipwreck-hunters now deploy an intriguing combination of old and new technology. Sonar and ultrasound gizmos have opened up breathtaking possibilities, yet the role of the backroom researcher, poring over ancient charts, checking shipping registers, and analyzing cargo lists has never been so important.

The amateur shipwreck enthusiast might be forgiven for envisioning the ocean floor as some kind of archeological theme park in which assorted craft through the ages are handily dotted about waiting to be discovered. Even the statistics look promising. Records show that half of all the sailing ships operating out of British ports in the 18th and 19th centuries were lost at sea. More than one fifth of these sank in deep water, suggesting that the rest lie on   reasonably accessible inshore sites.

In the 1860s a total of 2,537 U.K. ships sank in deep water and, according to Lloyd's of London, one thousand of the 10,000 ships insured between 1864 and 1869 were lost without trace. If the odds on any one ship sinking are applied to estimates of the number of vessels built during the 1st millennium BC, it is reasonable to conclude that more than 15,000 went down in either the Mediterranean or the Black Sea. If the figures were to take into account that 19th century ships were stronger, and possessed better charts and navigational aids, the actual number of ancient European wrecks is likely to be far greater.

The reality, of course, is that locating any particular wreck demands a combination of patience, skill, a huge investment, a willingness to gamble, and a large slice of luck. Popular hunting grounds are determined by two principal factors: established trading routes and areas afflicted by particularly vicious weather conditions. The Carribean, for instance, with its combination of swift currents, raging hurricanes, and an underwater maze of reefs claimed many vessels from the 15th century onward. The same is true of the typhoon-afflicted South China Sea, the Sea of Japan, Bay of Biscay, and deep-water areas of the Indian Ocean. The northeastern coast of North America is a notorious winter graveyard for ships.

ABOVE: Samuel Plimsoll. The overloading of unseaworthy ships was a common practice until the British Board of Trade adopted the recommendation of Plimsoll in 1876. He decreed that every ship should bear a line on the hull so that inspectors could see when it was laden to an acceptable level and no further. Parliament passed this as the Load Line Act, but ever since it has been known as the "Plimsoll Line."

The problems for sail-powered vessels were (and are) legion. Ships can be blown over by storm-force gales or, in running before the wind, find themselves ploughing into the sheer backside of a wave with catastrophic results. A sudden switch in wind direction, for example beneath a weather front, can result in a ship being blown over backward. Falling masts can rip the heart out of the superstructure, while pounding waves on deck may remove hatch covers and allow water to pour below. Riding out a heavy swell in old, timber vessels has always been a high-risk business, especially where the ballasting is wrong or the hull unsound. If planking flexes too much beneath a wave's crest and trough, then caulking seams fall apart and the ship starts to founder.

Sadly, for nervous early mariners, the above hazards were only the start. Inexperienced navigators, drunken shipmasters, fires caused by spilled oil lamps or glowing cooking coals, attacks by pirates or enemy warships, and the ruthlessness of wreckers (more of which later) were all part and parcel of life at sea. Just as dangerous were the shorebased owners who determined that masters should not waste cargo space. The overloading of ships was common practice until the British Board of Trade adopted the recommendation of the M.P. Samuel Plimsoll, who decreed that every vessel should bear lines showing when the hull was laden to a safe maximum. These lines typically covered operation in salt or freshwater, tropical

BELOW: *The Sea of Darkness*, by Olaus Magnus. This woodcut of a sea snake from 1555 shows the superstitious fear of mariners in centuries past. With so many losses at sea, tales of monsters and enchantments were taken very seriously indeed. In reality, early seafarers were beset by a number of dangers including unseaworthiness of the vessel, overloading, inexperience, fire, attack by enemies, drunkeness on board, as well as the perils of the weather and badly charted rocks.

RIGHT: The Colossus of Rhodes, one of the Seven Wonders of the World, is believed to have carried a light to guide mariners. The statue is of the god Helios and despite legend, which maintains that the huge statue stood astride the entrance to the harbor, it was probably built to one side.

BELOW: The Pharos Lighthouse of Alexandria, another of the Seven Wonders of the World. This monumental prototype lighthouse was completed in about 280 B.C. and was roughly 400 ft. (122 m.) high. The light arrangement of a fire reflected by mirrors was supposedly designed by Archimedes and could be seen for about 30 miles (48 km.).

or northern seas, and winter and summer sailings. Parliament passed the necessary laws under the 1876 Merchant Shipping Act but this particular feature on a hull still goes by its colloquial name—the "Plimsoll Line."

There is no doubt that shipping losses were a major concern of early sea-faring rulers. The Pharos of Alexandria, one of the Seven ancient Wonders of the World, was a 440 ft. (135 m.) high beacon built to guide ships safely to the entrance of the Egyptian port. It was finished around 280 B.C. for Ptolemy II of Egypt and became a model for other early lighthouses throughout the Mediterranean. The Colossus of Rhodes, another of the world's Seven Wonders, dating from the same period, was a 100 ft. (30 m.) bronze statue of the sun-god Helios. There is some evidence that this was also a light-bearing monument until it was destroyed by an earthquake 50 years after completion.

Although there is archeological evidence of transoceanic voyages by pre-historic sailors, the first truly epic journeys of the northern seas were made by Vikings. In their superbly designed craft they traveled to Britain, Ireland, Iceland, and Greenland, relying on a thorough navigational knowledge of the sun, moon, and stars and a finely-honed instinct for dead reckoning. Most scholars now accept that it was the Vikings, rather than Christopher Columbus, who discovered North America, though it is anyone's guess as to how many brave crews perished in the process. Today, our knowledge of the Vikings has been vastly assisted by the discovery of ship burials, in which deceased kings were interred in the vessels they commanded.

By the Middle Ages, it was the British, Spanish, and Portugeuse adventurers who were navigating unchartered waters, exploiting hitherto undreamed of wealth in the New World. Men such as Sir Francis Drake, whose circumnavigation of the world in 1580 produced enough treasure to create the English Navy; Columbus, who commandeered huge amounts of gold from the Americas; and Vasco da Gama, who helped found Portugal's empire in the Indian Ocean all played their part in establishing the European superpowers. From this point on it was clear to all rulers with colonial ambitions that naval might was paramount.

As new lands were discovered, so rivalry and the potential for conflict increased—a scenario well illustrated by the French Revolutionary Wars in the Caribbean during the late 19th century. Though this book avoids wrecks caused by act of war, it is worth mentioning that the protracted Carribean tussle between the British and French resulted in a loss of shipping on a scale previously unseen. Attacks on an enemy's merchant navy now emerged as a key aspect of war at sea and both sides began shepherding trading vessels within trans-Atlantic naval convoys.

Throughout the 1700s, trade routes, both east and west, grew ever busier. Shippers such as the British East India Company prospered on the transport of tea, spices, and silk from the Far East, pepper from Sumatra and India, cinnamon from Ceylon, and precious stones and carpets from Persia,

FAR LEFT: Sir Francis Drake, England's flamboyant buccaneer. Drake was the most famous seaman of the Elizabethan age: in addition to his victories over the Spanish he was celebrated as the first sailor to circumnavigate the globe.

LEFT: Daniel Defoe whose *Tour Through Great Britain* exposed the deadly work of "wreckers" on the remote coasts of Devon and Cornwall. These unscrupulous villains would lure ships onto the rocks with false lights in order to loot the wreck. Any survivors would be murdered as the law stated that the booty only became common property if all lives aboard were lost.

LEFT: Antique wood statues at Marquesas Key, Florida, hold treasure from the shipwreck of the *Santa Margarita* near the site of the ship's sinking, 24 miles (38 km.) off Key West. The statues were made in the 1590s, at the time of the wreck.

Indonesia, and China. The Dutch, too, were establishing a reputation as a long-range trading nation, their fast three-masted clippers unlocking the vast treasures of the Orient to the delight of the European gentry.

Little wonder that, in many a coastal town and village, the poor would eye such magnificent vessels and quietly wonder when the next gale might drive one ashore. Such thoughts were particularly prevalent in Britain where a Common Law "Right Of Wreck" allowed anyone to claim legal title to goods and artifacts genuinely salvaged from the sea. On the Isles of Scilly, a storm-lashed group of islands in the Western Approaches, local parsons would sometimes offer up the following prayer on behalf of their poverty-stricken flock: "Dear Lord, if it be thy will that ships must come to grief, then let it be that they come to grief on Scilly."

The problem for would-be salvagers was that finding lucrative wrecks was down to pure chance. Villages could go half a century or more without a ship driving in on their "patch." Inevitably, some unscrupulous types decided that the masters of passing vessels needed a little assistance to guide them onto the rocks. This was the heyday of the wreckers and, particularly on the wild and rugged coasts of Devon and Cornwall, they had the perfect environment in which to ply their grim trade. For one thing the Bristol Channel was then the busiest shipping lane in the world. For another the coast was a notorious ship's graveyard, buffeted all year by sudden and vicious storms. Importantly it was also remote, far from the prying eyes of the Customs men or the King's soldiery.

The wreckers used a simple yet devastatingly effective method of luring shipping onto rocks. Lighthouses and lightships had been around since King Henry VIII's time. (He granted a royal charter to Trinity House, the country's lighthouse and pilotage authority in 1514.) Mariners relied heavily on them to steer a safe coastal course on stormy nights. Knowing this, the wreckers would extinguish a genuine light and substitute their own in a suitably treacherous position. Or they would mimick the lights of local harbors by placing lanterns on the clifftop. Sometimes these false lights would be attached to the tails of horses and donkeys and frequently moved to further confuse the hapless victims out at sea.

Legally, if anyone (even a dog) escaped alive from a wrecked ship, it was not considered open to plunder. Consequently, this sealed the fate of any half-drowned seaman or passenger who managed to drag him or herself ashore. No wrecker was going to have a good night's work ruined by the tenacity of his victims. The slaughter of such unfortunates was a regular occurrence, alluded to by writers such as Daniel Defoe in his *Tour Through Great Britain*. Defoe wrote of ". . . the sands covered in people, they are charged with strange bloody and cruel dealings, even sometimes with one another, but especially the poor distressed seamen who seek for help for their lives and find the rocks themselves not more cruel and merciless than the people who range about them for their prey."

ABOVE: The wreck of the *Agnes C. Donohoe*, lost off the coast of Nova Scotia, Canada. Often lying just beneath the surface, razor sharp rocks can bring catastrophe upon the unwary or the incautious.

INSET RIGHT: The falling tide can leave an unwary ship stranded. Luckily, this survey vessel was able to be rescued and repaired.

RIGHT: The *City of Paris*, October 13, 1901. While docked for the winter at Bergman on the Koyukuk River in Alaska, thieves looking for liquor boarded the vessel and set her on fire. The steamer burned to the waterline.

As the 19th century progressed the shipping industry was transformed by a series of major technical innovations. Steam power was harnessed to create wooden-hulled paddle steamers. Iron-built ships began to emerge with powerful screw-propellers that improved both speed and stability. Gradually the realization dawned that ocean travel could be promoted as a luxury form of travel far removed from the harsh, uncomfortable passages so typical of the age of sail. For the rich, voyages to the far colonies of Australia, India, South Africa, and Canada opened up a whole new decadent lifestyle combining travel, social etiquette, adventure, and entrepreneurial expansion. Shipping lines such as White Star and Cunard competed to provide the best restaurants, the finest champagne, and the most luxurious internal fittings. For the poor, often emigrating out of necessity, life in steerage class was far more basic, though still a vast improvement on the creaking, leaky wooden hulls of earlier years.

The loss of the "unsinkable" *Titanic* on her maiden voyage in 1912 did little to assuage enthusiasm for the passenger liner. Indeed, of the hundreds of liners plying the oceans, it is surprising that worldwide losses in the early years of the century were relatively slight. Of the 46 that went down between 1900 and 1910, 34 were by groundings (usually in fog), seven collided, two burned, two disappeared without trace, and one was sunk by a cyclone. During the following decade, passenger ship losses were reduced to 38, although the actual death toll climbed steeply to 5,165, of which 1,392 deaths were linked to enemy action. It was only with the onset of the 1920s, and peace among major world powers, that the casualty figures returned to typical levels; 21 ships lost or written off over the decade and 1,085 passengers and crew killed. By the 1950s the statistics had improved to such an extent that although more passengers than ever sailed the oceans, the actual number of fatalaties in ten years was just 157.

There was a combination of factors that helped achieve this. Development of radar and depth-gauging sonar theoretically allowed navigators to steer a safe course in all but the most severe weather conditions. And with so many more ships afloat, linked by more powerful

BELOW: Three crew died in the burning Norwegian oil tanker *Artemis* after she was in a collision with another vessel near Rotterdam. The ship was eventually completely burned out.

radios, the chance of a quick response to any Mayday signal was much improved. That said, the size of hulls—particularly those of commercial carriers—presented a new set of problems.

Disasters at sea now produced devastating environmental consequences, sometimes scarring vast areas of coastline for years. Wrecked oil tankers such as the *Torrey Canyon* (1967), the *Amoco Cadiz* (1978), and the *Exxon Valdez* (1989) proved timely reminders of the essential frailty of all ships.

Despite advances in navigation and communication, there remains an aura of mystery and danger about certain parts of the world. The so-called Bermuda Triangle, in the eastern Atlantic, has acquired a reputation as a graveyard for both ships and planes, dozens of which have apparently vanished without a trace. Even today there is talk of sea monsters, aliens, and unexplained forces capable of overwhelming vessels in seconds.

Much of this theorizing is highly speculative and conveniently ignores the fact that the seas around Bermuda are, in any case, among the most dangerous and volatile on the planet. However, many scientists do accept that anomalies in the Earth's magnetic field can produce unusually violent weather conditions and play havoc with modern navigational instruments.

For today's wreck hunter, the waters surrounding Bermuda and the Florida Keys probably contain the most valuable historical cargos in the world. The obvious difficulty comes in tracking down precise sites. Contemporary reports of a sinking are all very well, but a ship in trouble may have drifted for miles in high winds and strong currents before finally succumbing to the inevitable. Even when a wreck is located, the process of positively identifying it is nightmarish.

When the *Nuestra Senora de Atocha* sank off the Florida Keys in 1622, she was as richly laden a galleon as ever left the New World for Spain. Within days of her demise, the Spanish had a diving operation underway to salvage as many silver and gold ingots, jewels, coin strongboxes, and ornaments as they could. They met with little success. Much of the loot sunk quickly in the shifting sands and divers submerging on a single breath of air had no chance of working at speed. Resigned to their loss, Spanish officials drew up detailed charts and records in the hope that a fuller salvage operation could one day be undertaken. Finding and identifying the *Atocha* would be a source of great pleasure to a resourceful 20th century wreck hunter.

So it seemed in 1985 when a former Indiana chicken farmer called Mel Fisher discovered huge quantities of treasure just off the Florida Keys. He brought up an estimated $50 million worth of goods, exhibited much of it in a local museum, boosted the local tourist trade, and became an overnight hero. That should have been the end of the matter but another salvage man, Sam Kirby, then turned up claiming Fisher had got his calculations all wrong and that the real *Atocha* was lying 50 ft. (15 m.) down in a com-

RIGHT: This wreck, on the Skeleton Coast in Africa, clearly shows the damage that can be done by a collision with rocks. The hull of the vessel has been ripped wide open. It now provides a convenient nesting site for local seabirds.

RIGHT: A diver explores the wreck of an unidentified vessel. Diving for pleasure is currently enjoying a boom as scuba equipment becomes safer and more easily available, and the popularity of diving onto wrecks, in particular, is increasing. Many are now tourist attractions which are annually visited by hundreds of amateur divers.

pletely different location 14 miles (22 km.) off the Keys. As in other areas of archeology, the provenance of a wreck is a rare and precious thing!

It would be so much easier if they remained intact. Wooden wrecks can crumble away within a generation, the speed of the process governed by a number of variables. Firstly, there is the effect of long-term immersion in salt water and the extent to which the temperature of the sea influences chemical reactions. (Every decrease of 10°F/-12°C roughly halves the speed of a hull's degradation.) Even more destructive are the tiny marine boring organisms known as teredos, or shipworms. Their larvae bore into wood on touch, creating a pinhole-size entry, and once inside work along the grain hollowing out tunnels about one-third of an inch wide. According to U.S. Navy research, a typical wooden wreck can be completely devoured within 50 years, unless it is protected by mud or lying so deep that the water contains insufficient oxygen for worms to survive.

On this basis, the warm Mediterranean and Aegean Seas are unlikely to yield an intact ancient wreck, although the Black Sea, with its negligible deep-water oxygen count holds great promise for the future. Here, the water has a dense population of a bacteria called microspira, which liberates large amounts of poisonous hydrogen sulphide. As a result no animals have lived near the seabed for centuries; a conclusion obvious from the undisturbed layers of sediments. The chances are that sunken ships, some thousands of years old, are intact and their cargos perfectly preserved. Cloth, food, even human bodies could one day be recovered to give archeologists a stunning insight into the lifestyle of these ill-fated crews.

So what of the future? There can be no doubt that technological advances have given wreck hunters a crucial, if expensive, edge. These days, salvage teams will typically use satellite global positioning aids to program an onboard computer's seabed search area. The computer produces an on-screen grid dividing the ocean floor into lines 657 ft. (200 m.) apart, which can be systematically searched with incredible accuracy. Directional propellers will keep a salvager within 10 ft. (3 m.) of his programmed course, while a "torpedo" carrying magnetometers is towed behind, bombarding the seabed with a 1,313 ft. (400 m.) wide beam of sonar signals.

All objects longer than 5 ft. (1.5 m.) can be recorded and relayed instantly onto chart-room screens together with the topography of the seabed. Ultrasound scanners, designed to penetrate up to 263 ft. (80 m.) into sand are then directed at potentially interesting shapes to establish whether they are pieces of wreckage. In good conditions, a well-trained team can cover 0.6 sq. miles/hr (1.5 sq. km./hr)—breathtaking speed in comparison to the anchor-and-hope methods of the early treasure seekers.

Once a wreck is discovered, the process of salvage—particularly on deep-water sites—remains a delicate business. Yet even here, science has eased the burden. Mini-submarines capable of accessing virtually any depth of water, self-propelled cameras, which can be steered from a joystick on

ABOVE: January 3, 1962. The *Flying Enterprise* which is listing up to 80° in raging seas. The captain of the vessel, Kurt Carlsen, was the only survivor. Rescue attempts were hampered by the fierce storm which caused the ship to founder.

RIGHT: Hundreds of people died when a train ferry capsized near Hakdate, Japan, in a typhoon on October 6, 1964.

the surface, robot "grabs" equipped to recover 5,000 lb. (2,270 kg.) items and gas lifting bags designed to raise entire chunks of hull have become everyday weapons in the salvager's armory. Given an unlimited budget and plenty of time, few wrecks are now considered impossible targets.

In some ways it is the greatest of them all, the *Titanic*, which has provided marine archeology with this springboard into the millennium. From the moment it was found by geologist Dr. Robert Ballard in 1985, and later filmed for Hollywood's biggest-ever movie blockbuster, this grand old ship has unlocked doors throughout government, academia, and the military. Without this triumph on his resume, it is unlikely that Ballard would have been allowed to borrow one of the U.S. Navy's most advanced atomic submarines, built to recover highly sensitive defense equipment. This NR1 sub, which can roll on wheels across the seabed, has enabled Ballard to follow ancient Mediterranean trade routes; literally driving among some of the oldest lost ships in the world. The potential for other unexplored wreck sites is virtually limitless.

Slowly, the sea is giving up her secrets. In the years ahead, shipwrecks will rewrite history.

RIGHT: This is a classic image from literature, an illustration from the first edition of *Robinson Crusoe* by Daniel Defoe, showing Robinson Crusoe saving goods from the wreck of his ship.

LEFT: An unidentified vessel illustrates the danger of rocky coastlines. This ship was lost on the rocks off Slea Head in County Kerry, Ireland. Rocks are one of the greatest hazards faced by shipping. Mariners have charted these hidden hazards over the years to the extent that, in theory, no ship should come to grief. However, tidal flow, currents, wind, weather, and human error can still bring a ship to grief on the rocks.

SHIPWRECKS

Kyrenia ship

288 B.C.
Cyprus

Little is known of the seafarers' lot in ancient times. It's only thanks to the chance discovery of a wreck lying off the coast of Cyprus in 30 ft. (9 m.) of water that we can draw any conclusions with certainty. More than half the body of the Kyrenia remained intact when it was found in 1967, over 2,200 years after going down.

Eight years later the timbers were raised and restored. Some of the goods aboard survived as well, among them harvested almonds, kitchenware, cloth, amphoras, and ingots. Sailors of the era, it seems, relied heavily on fishing for food, had no stove aboard, and patched up their vessels after attacks by timber worm. There appear to have been four sailors aboard and the presence of iron spearheads in the side of the boat suggests an attack, possibly by pirates, in which the crew were most likely captured and sold as slaves, and the boat scuttled.

Kinneret boat

1st century A.D.
Sea of Galilee

The wreck of the Kinneret boat was found buried in mud on the shoreline of the Sea of Galilee. This was similar to vessels used in Jesus' time by his apostles. It is impossible to glean anything of the lifestyle of the sailors who used it. There's speculation that the boat might have been wrecked in a battle between Jews and Romans in 67 A.D. in which the native forces were wiped out.

The White Ship

November 25, 1120
Off Cherbourg, France

According to chronicler William of Malmesbury: "No ship ever brought so much misery to England. None was ever so notorious in the history of the world." The White Ship—or to give it the correct title *Blanche Nef*—sailed from Barfleur, near Cherbourg in France, as part of a royal flotilla. On board were William and Richard, the only legitimate sons of King Henry I (1070-

PREVIOUS PAGE: The *Paris* on fire in the port of Le Havre, 1939.

RIGHT: The *Mary Rose* was the pride of England's fleet and a magnificent looking ship. Her loss was due to bad design; the shipbuilders made gunports far too low in her hull, allowing water to spill in when she listed in a squall.

BELOW: The salvaged *Mary Rose* is a treasure trove of artifacts; a preserved microcosm of Tudor society. In this picture floating cranes lift her remains to the surface for the first time in over 400 years. This piece of the hull is now the central attraction at an excellent *Mary Rose* exhibition in Portsmouth, England.

1135). Henry is remembered as a sound but licentious king. He fathered an estimated 20 illegitimate sons and countless illegitimate daughters; among them Maud, Countess of Perche, who also sailed in the White Ship. The voyage got underway after some merry-making—perhaps that's why the ship's master inadvertently guided the vessel onto the notorious rocks in the English Channel known as Le Raz de Catteville.

Prince William escaped in a small boat but was touched by the cries of his half sister Maud, still aboard the foundering ship. He returned for her and died in a brave but foolhardy rescue attempt. The sole survivor was Berold, a tradesman, who clung to the sail ropes of the stricken ship and was picked up by fishermen the next morning. After King Henry learned of the disaster it was said he never smiled again. Intriguingly, Stephen, cousin of the drowned princes, decided at the last moment not to take passage on the White Ship and went onto claim the throne of England.

Mary Rose

1545
Off Portsmouth, Great Britain

Foundering is a problem that has affected mariners for centuries. In the mid-16th century the *Mary Rose*, flagship and pride of King Henry VIII's navy, complete with a crew of 400, sailed out into the Solent, off England's south coast, with the aim of fighting the French. However, on her maiden voyage she was caught in a sudden squall. She heeled over to port, and water poured in through her open lower gun ports. The ship filled up and sank within minutes.

Spanish Armada

1588
Around the shores of Great Britain

One of the earliest maritime tragedies to cause huge loss of life followed the decision of King Philip II of Spain to invade England and overthrow the Protestant Queen, Elizabeth I, for the greater glory of Spain and the Catholic church. In 1586, encouraged by Pope Pius V, Philip instructed the Marques de Santa Cruz to gather together a huge armada so that the invasion could commence. The plan would have proceeded earlier in the century, but Sir Francis Drake, England's naval hero, crippled the Spanish in 1567 with his usual flamboyance by sailing into the port of Cadiz and burning half of the Spanish fleet. The English laughed at how easily Drake

ABOVE: A scene of conflict and fire as the Spanish Armada is defeated by the English fleet. The Spanish were out-gunned and out-maneuvered by the fast English ships and were forced to make their escape around the cold and treacherous seas off Scotland.

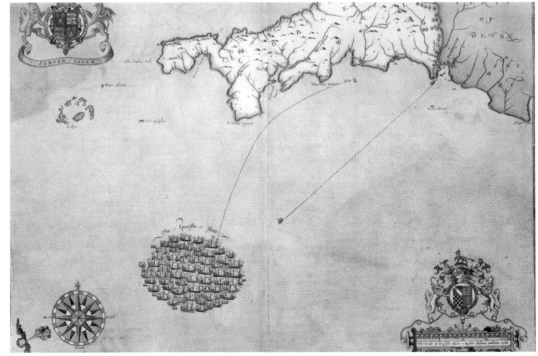

RIGHT: This map from c. 1588 charts the position of the Spanish Armada off the south-west coast of England. In all, 63 ships of the Armada now lie on the seabed around Britain. Those that eventually managed to limp home to Spain were a lesson in Britain's naval superiority.

RIGHT: Legend has it that the cool and confident Drake refused to set sail against the Spanish until he had finished his game of bowls.

had "singed the King of Spain's beard." Furious and determined, the Spanish rebuilt their warships, and in May 1588 a flotilla of 130, carrying 30,000 soldiers and sailors, left Lisbon on a mission to conquer England. Under the command of Don Alonzo Perez de Guzman, the Duke of Medina Sidonia, they planned to meet the Duke of Parma in Flanders, combine forces, and simply overwhelm the English.

Bad weather in the English Channel and the cannons of Drake's English ships soon had the formidable fleet in disarray however. The Spanish were dealt a crushing defeat from a fleet half their size off the coast of France. In confusion they missed their rendezvous in Flanders and set off to escape the Channel by heading east. Medina Sidonia, an inexpert seaman, set out to sail around the north of Scotland and return home to Spain via the west coast of Ireland—a monumental journey through hostile waters. His flagship, the *Gran Grifon*, was one of many to perish during the foolhardy voyage and foundered on the rocks of Fair Isle taking 1,000 men to the bottom. Many of the other ships were already in a poor condition—leaking like sieves and full of cannon holes—and the increasingly wintry weather claimed its fair share of victims. Among the unluckiest were those under the command of Admiral Alonso Martinez de Leyva. Having lost the *Santa Ana* and *La Rata Santa Maria Encoronado* off Donegal, the admiral put his surviving men to work patching up the galley *Girona* in the harbor at Killybegs, Ireland. They did a thorough job, patching up the hull and decks, rebuilding her masts and loading cannons, provisions, and 1,300 men.

Consequently, she set sail for Spain on October 26, 1588, and the following day was overwhelmed by an enormous hurricane. *Girona* foundered and every one of the 1,300 men on board, including the admiral, were drowned. In all, 63 ships of the Spanish Armada sank, taking with them anywhere from 4,000 to 10,000 men. The 65 ships that did make it home were all in a sorry state.

Nuestra Senora de Atocha

September 4, 1622
Florida Keys, U.S.A.

The three masted *Atocha* was the flagship of the small fleet which came out of Florida bound for Spain. She was laden with treasure including gems, silver jewelry, and gold ingots when she went down with eight other ships and 550 men. It is one of history's earliest salvage stories as immediately after the catastrophe, divers tried to retrieve the cargo, which had been pilfered from settlements in the New World. They had limited success as the shifting sands soon laid claim to the booty. However, those early salvagers made detailed notes of their efforts and it is these charts that have inspired today's

treasure hunters to relocate the wreck site. The original documents pay tribute to one slave who was so dedicated in his efforts to dive for the treasure that he was given his freedom as a reward.

Blessing of Burntisland

July 10, 1633
Firth of Forth, Great Britain

A trip by Charles I (1600-1649) to Scotland for a formal coronation ended up as a personal disaster when royal treasures plunged to the bottom of the Firth of Forth. Little is known of the foray into Scotland by the ill-fated English king, which occurred some 15 years before he was beheaded at Whitehall. He and his entourage had spent several months touring Scotland visiting palaces and towns and collecting celebration gifts en route. The king was to travel from Burntisland by the royal man-of-war, the *Dreadnought,* anchored in the waters of the Firth. Two ferries set off from the port to reach the ship. Only one arrived. While the king was safely delivered, the second ferry was overwhelmed by a sudden storm. Horrified, the king watched as it capsized. Not only was his concern for the 35 friends and servants who lost their lives that day but also for the royal belongings that hit the bottom. One estimate put the 17th century value of the lost treasure at $160,000 (£100,000), about a sixth of the nation's wealth. Among the valuables lost was a 250-piece silver dining service. In order that the event could not be construed as a bad omen, a group of witches was tried for causing the catastrophe and executed.

Nuestra Senora de las Maravillas

January 4, 1656
Bahamas

The wreck of the *Maravillas* is remembered not only as an underwater treasure trove but also for the vivid description of the ship's dark last moments bequeathed to the U.S. by a surviving priest. Don Diego Portichelo de Ribadenevra, keeper of the Holy Metropolitan Church in Lima, was one of 45 passengers who was saved out of the 650 returning to Spain from Havana. After a navigational error sent the ship onto a bank, Ribadenevra gave the following account to an inquiry in Castile.

"The confusion of the people was so great that they did not realize the importance of the sails to get them out of the danger, and instead occupied

themselves in trying to stem the flow of the water pouring into the ship.

"With the sails idle, the currents rapidly drove the ship toward the banks. She bumped against the rocks so forcefully that her seams began to crack. Though the people were bailing with four pumps and pails, the water rose as high as the second deck.

"Up to that time I heard confessions from many people, among them Admiral Don Matias de Orellana who told me that we would surely die and that I should grant absolution to everyone."

The priest and two others used a hatch as a life raft.

"They even took off their shirts and I took mine off with so much difficulty that I finally had to tear it off. There I was, left in my underpants, the crucifix that I had brought with me in my hand. At that time I heard a voice saying: 'Is there some priest that can absolve me, because I have been the greatest sinner in the world?'

"I stood up on the hatch cover with some difficulty. My companions held me by the belt of my underpants. I don't know how I suddenly found myself forgetting about the danger I was in. I raised my voice and told them: 'Here is a priest. Say now: I sinned, my Lord God, and I shall absolve you.'"

The priest and his companions were plucked from the sea at dawn by a rescue ship. "I began to sing *Te Deum Laudamus*—at the same time crying so hard that I could barely articulate the verses."

French Fleet

May 11, 1678
Venezuela

A French fleet of 35 ships carrying 6,000 men aiming to invade the Dutch-held Curacao Island was smashed on coral reefs surrounding islands off the Venezuelan coast.

On the night of the disaster some 18 ships went down, taking with them 500 men. A further 2,500 men were marooned on islands close to where the fleet had foundered. Their ordeal was only just beginning—nearly half succumbed to the ravages of starvation and disease on the islands before French rescue ships arrived three months later.

Recently divers have discovered the site of nine of the shipwrecks. The fleet flagship, the *Terrible*, which had 70 guns and a 15 ft. (5 m.) anchor, still has pistols, swords, and coins aboard. Reports have come back of bronze cannons piled up "like a stack of logs" on the sea bed.

RIGHT: A marine excavator holds gold dubloons found in the wreck of the Spanish ship *Nuestra Senora de las Maravillas*, which was lost off the Bahamas in the 17th century.

RIGHT: The *Association* comes to grief on the notorious rocks off the Scilly Islands in 1707. This particularly treacherous region has claimed the lives of a countless number of mariners over the centuries. On this occasion the incompetence of the commander, Sir Cloudesly Shovel, caused the loss of about 1,650 souls.

H.M.S. *Association*

October 22, 1707
Scilly Isles, Great Britain

RIGHT AND BELOW RIGHT: These two etchings show the sinking of the *Royal George* which was holed by rocks off Spithead, Isle of Wight, in 1782.

When their role in the Siege of Toulon in France was finished, a British fleet comprising a dozen ships of the line, three lesser ships, a sloop, a yacht, and four fireships headed for home under the command of Sir Cloudesley Shovel.

Shovel—and the majority of his sailing masters—became confused over their exact position and instead of sailing up the English Channel they steered onto the notorious rocks of the Scillies. The lead ship H.M.S. *Association* was lost with all hands. Moments later the same fate befell the *Eagle*. One man out of the entire crew survived on the *Romney* and 25 were saved from the fireship *Firebrand*. The casualty list was about 1,650—rivaling that at the Battle of Trafalgar, one of the most famous sea battles in history. Shovel, who has since been berated for his navigational ineptitude was among those who perished. His body was washed up on Porth Hellick in the Scillies; local folklore has it that he was alive when he was first washed up and that a woman confessed on her death bed to murdering him for his rings. Shovel was first buried just above the high tide line but his body was disinterred a few days later and removed to Westminster Abbey. However, the bodies of the two step-sons who died with him and Edmund Loades, Captain of the Fleet, were buried at an island church.

English Armada

1711
Labrador, Canada

Plans to capture Quebec for England came to a tragic end when an English armada foundered. A fleet of 61 warships and transports carrying nearly 10,000 British sailors and troops with their families was heading for Quebec at the end of April carrying sealed orders from Queen Anne to capture the heavily-armed fortress city. They stopped first in Boston to load provisions before heading up the Massachusetts coast for the St. Lawrence. The fleet captured a French sloop, the *Neptune*, on the way and, with unbelievable stupidity, Admiral Sir Hovenden Walker, in command, decided its skipper, Captain Paradis, a Frenchman, would pilot them through the difficult waters of St. Lawrence Bay. When heavy fog descended on August 22, Paradis guided the fleet into a particularly treacherous zone near Egg Island. Eight transporter ships were dashed against the razor-sharp reefs and more than

2,000 people were swept into the black, freezing waters. Paradis disappeared and, without enough troops remaining to continue the attack, Walker gathered his remaining ships together and turned for home. Evidence was later discovered that some of the shipwrecked victims managed to find their way onto Egg Island, but none were thought to have survived long enough to leave.

Diana

March 5, 1817
Malaya

The *Diana* was one of countless ships that sank in bad weather with all hands lost. Today, the East India Company ship has become remarkable for yielding her treasures nearly two centuries after going under. Laden with valuables gathered in Canton, China, the squarerigged ship was calling in at Calcutta before heading for Amsterdam when she got caught in a storm in the Strait of Malacca, between Malaya and Sumatra. Hidden rocks did their worst and the ship went down in 100 ft. (30 m.) of water.

Diver Dorian Bell spent three years pinpointing the wreck and in December 1993 he finally got to grips with the lost cargo. Although little remained of the wooden ship, Dorian and his team recovered 23,821 pieces of porcelain as well as beads, marble, and bottles of port.

Essex

November 20, 1820
South Atlantic

When novelist Herman Melville (1819-91) wrote his masterpiece *Moby Dick,* he was inspired not only through his own adventures on the high seas but also the tale told to him by fellow whaler Owen Chase. Chase was first mate of the *Essex* whaleship, one of 100 such vessels during the first half of the 19th century that came out of Nantucket, the island off Massachusetts, the heart of America's whaling industry. It was a hazardous business, as Chase testified. "The profession is one of great ambition. A tame man is never known among them and the coward is marked with that peculiar aversion that distinguishes our public naval service." The epic voyage began on August 12, under the captaincy of George Pollock Jr. with a crew of 20 aboard. Men were at sea for months at a time pursuing whales, and it was in November that they encountered one that would shape their destiny.

The hunters were cast off in a small boat when they harpooned a whale in the expanses of the South Pacific. It retaliated and they were unable to bring in a catch. Soon afterward, with the men back on the main ship, a terrifying scene suddenly began to unfold. A whale of some 85 ft. (26 m.) in length appeared and began to ram the ship. In Owen's words:

"He spouted two or three times and then disappeared. In less than two or three seconds he came up again, about the length of the ship off, and made directly for us at the rate of about three knots.

"I could distinctly see him smite his jaws together, as if distracted with rage and fury."

The impact of two charges by the whale was enough to flood the lower compartments of the ship. When the whale left, the captain and crew had no choice but to take to three small boats. They were 1,000 miles (1,600 km.) from land with only limited supplies of food and water. It was weeks before they were rescued by a passing ship, by which time a dozen men had perished.

Washington

May 14, 1831
Long Island Sound, U.S.A.

Two people lost their lives when the six-year-old paddle steamer *Washington* collided with the *Chancellor Livingstone* in Long Island Sound.

Caledonia

1842
North Cornwall, Great Britain

A lonely white figurehead standing in a remote churchyard in Cornwall, England, is a lasting tribute to nine men who lost their lives when the 200 ton *Caledonia* was wrecked in foul weather on the rocks at Sharp's Nose, Morwenstow, North Cornwall. The ship was on its way home to Scotland with a cargo of wheat from Odessa on the Black Sea when it was brought to grief by the storm. Only one crew member survived. The lifeless figurehead is from the doomed ship.

Lady Elgin

September 8, 1851
Waukegan, Illinois, U.S.A.

More than 280 people died when the *Lady Elgin*, a 1,000 ton paddle steamer built in 1851, collided with the schooner *Augusta* of Waukegan, Illinois.

Birkenhead

1852
The Cape, South Africa

The wreck of the *Birkenhead* is remembered for the courage and outstanding discipline of the soldiers aboard. The *Birkenhead* put out from Cork in Ireland with almost 650 soldiers aboard, many accompanied by their young families. Their destination was South Africa. The voyage was all but over when a storm enveloped the vessel as it approached the Cape. The captain miscalculated as he sought calmer waters and brought the ship too close to the rocks where she was holed. Soon after the impact a young bugler called the recruits on parade where they struggled to keep in ranks on the tilting deck. The outlook was bleak. Although the beach was close by, the seas were mountainous and there was only one boat to take off survivors. The soldiers stood to attention until the *Birkenhead* began to break up. Only then did their officers order them to "abandon ship." The waters were infested with sharks however, and only 184 soldiers reached the shore. The "*Birkenhead* drill" was thereafter dispatched to folklore and history as an example of good soldierly conduct.

Pennsylvania

1858
Mississippi

Before finding fame as a writer, Mark Twain was Samuel Clemens, of Hannibal, Missouri, a boatman. He was an apprentice pilot on the steamboat *Pennsylvania*, and his younger brother, Henry, was a clerk on the same vessel. When the boat was berthed at St. Louis, Samuel stayed at a boarding house, while Henry opted to remain aboard the boat. In a dream Samuel saw the body of his brother in a metal coffin propped on two chairs. On his chest was a bouquet of white flowers with a single crimson bloom at its center.

RIGHT: The *Birkenhead* goes down by the bows. This picture is from a contemporary newspaper illustration; the courage of all on board the ship was widely reported at the time.

RIGHT: On February 13, 1953, the *Queen Victoria* was en route from Liverpool, England, to Ireland. She was caught in a storm off the Bailey Lighthouse near Dublin and wrecked. The disaster claimed the lives of 67 people.

Disturbed by the vivid dream, Samuel nevertheless rejoined his brother for a trip downriver. In New Orleans the pair split, with Samuel joining the steamboat *Lacey*, which was to sail up river two days after the *Pennsylvania*. A few days later, grim news awaited Samuel when the *Lacey* reached Greenville, Mississippi. He was told that 150 people had died on the *Pennsylvania* following an explosion at Ship Island in Memphis. Samuel dashed to the scene and found his brother on the point of death. Following his demise, Samuel visited Henry's body. It was in a metal coffin that was resting on two chairs, just as it had been in the dream. Before his astonished eyes an elderly woman entered the makeshift mortuary and placed a bunch of white flowers with a single red rose at its heart on the chest of the dead boy.

U.S.S. *Monitor*

December 29, 1862
Cape Hatteras, U.S.A.

It's not the way the U.S.S. *Monitor* sank that excites interest today—the steamer went down while under tow by U.S.S. *Rhode Island* about half a mile from Cape Hatteras lighthouse without loss of life—it's the historical value now attached to the wreck, which has a wooden hull armored with eight-inch wrought-iron plate. The length of the *Monitor* was 172 ft. (53 m.) and its beam 41.5 ft. (13 m.).

Sultana

April 27, 1865
Memphis, Tennessee

The *Sultana* was a typical side-wheel steamboat, which plied a regular route between New Orleans and St. Louis shipping cotton. She was legally registered to carry 376 people, including crew. However, at the time of her last voyage, the south was full of Union Civil War veterans, most of them recently released from prisoner of war camps and all desperate to return home to the north. Consequently, when *Sultana* left her last port of call, Memphis, she was loaded with about 1,800 people—nearly five times her legal load. Soldiers crowded every space in the hull, some even sleeping in the pilot house, as she labored against a strong current up the Mississippi. Furthermore, she had recently been experiencing problems with a leaking boiler, which had been patched up to allow her to continue the voyage.

At 2.00 hours, the overworked boiler exploded, ripping a great rent in the boat and throwing sleeping soldiers into the icy waters—one survivor later told how he found himself thrown over 200 ft. (60 m.) from the ship, luckily falling into the river with only minor injuries. The blast from the explosion was heard in Memphis, which the *Sultana* had left two hours previously and boats immediately set out from the town to see what had happened. Meanwhile, the scene of the disaster was nightmarish. Men struggled in the water, showered by burning coals and pieces of wreckage, yet there was little for them to cling to and, weakened by their incarceration in the camps, they drowned in their hundreds. The remains of the *Sultana* soon caught ablaze, adding a new dimension of horror to events. Most survivors left aboard chose to jump into the already crowded waters to escape the rapidly growing inferno; many of those left on board were tipped into the flames by buckling decks.

The death toll of 1,600 is a conservative estimate. As no muster was taken when the eager soldiers scrambled up the gangplank, nobody will ever really know exactly how many died. Certainly, more than went down on the *Titanic*.

Ironically, news of America's most horrific and devastating shipwreck made little impact in the press at the time. News of the end of the war and the death of President Lincoln dominated the front pages and many staff in the higher eschelons of the army were keen to draw a veil over the episode.

RIGHT, ABOVE AND BELOW: A paddle-steamer built in 1863, the *Sultana* was ripped apart by a boiler explosion on the Mississippi River above Memphis. The loss of life was immense. About 1,600 people died.

Atlantic

April 1, 1873
Halifax, U.S.A.

The steamship *Atlantic* was part of the ill-fated White Star Line. She was wrecked with nearly 550 lives lost.

Princess Alice

September 1878
Woolwich, London, Great Britain

The weather was balmy, the waters were calm. No one could foretell the disaster that awaited the passengers of the paddle steamer *Princess Alice* as they took a trip around the Thames estuary on a Sunday afternoon. The tragedy came upon them suddenly. A mile from the landing stage at Woolwich Arsenal, a collier, *Bywell Castle*, began bearing down on the

LEFT AND BELOW LEFT: The *Princess Alice* was another paddle steamer which was wrecked with immense loss of life. Terror reigned following a collision with the giant collier *Bywell Castle* and within five minutes the pleasure boat had vanished beneath the calm waters of the Thames estuary, taking with her 650 souls.

LEFT: The aft of the *Princess Alice*, beached near Woolwich. The engines and paddle wheel boxes can be easily seen.

leisure cruiser. A mighty industrial giant, the *Bywell Castle* was six times bigger than the *Princess Alice* and effortlessly ripped her in two. All but 50 of the 700 people aboard died as the *Princess Alice* sank within five minutes of the collision.

Sunrise

June 19, 1882
Finisterre, Spain

One man saved 33 sailors and two 12-year-old children after their merchantman was smashed against the razor rocks at Finisterre in Spain.

Lucerne

November 17, 1886
Lake Superior

The schooner *Lucerne*, launched in 1873, was a staunch vessel, reflecting the $55,000 invested in her. There were ten crew aboard when she embarked on her last voyage carrying iron ore up the lake, captained by George Lloyd of Cleveland. The mate Robert Jeffreys was on his first trip.

Lucerne was last seen embattled with snow squalls and gale force winds. No one knows precisely what happened, but she was certainly overcome by the adverse weather. Wreckage was later discovered off the beach of Long Island, 60 miles (96 km.) west of where she was last sighted. The local lightkeeper recorded:

"From tower saw a vessel with two masts pretty close to shore. I went down. I found it was a barque wrecked. It appered that they had let go their anchors . . . I discovered three bodies, one in main, two in mizzen rigging. Did not find any bodies on shore."

The dead were taken to Ashland where, according to the Ashland weekly press, they were "embalmed by Henry Scott, who has preserved a wonderfully natural and lifelike appearance." Further bodies were later given up by the Lake, although four were never found.

Lucerne's hull remains intact and upright on a sand bottom 25 ft. (82 m.) down, its cargo of iron ore is still scattered around the wreck.

H.M.S. *Serpent*

November 10, 1890
Finisterre, Spain

Mystery surrounds the appalling tragedy of the H.M.S. *Serpent*, a Royal Navy school ship that foundered on the rocks at Finisterre one stormy November night. Only three sailors of the 175 aboard returned alive. Officially, the wreck was caused by a navigational accident exacerbated by pounding waves and gale-force winds.

Locally, the story goes that the *Serpent* was carrying gold to the army in South Africa. Forewarned Spanish wreckers lured the ill-fated vessel onto the rocks by turning off the local lighthouse, but so poor were weather conditions that even they, equipped with inside knowledge, could not reach the wreckage. There are claims that one chest of gold was recovered by a Royal Navy ship while another was hoarded by the Galicians living nearby.

Whatever the truth, the local beaches were strewn with dead bodies after the disaster and those in the village of Xavina did all they could for the three survivors. For years afterward the Royal Navy committed a crown of flowers to the sea at the spot where the *Serpent* was lost and until 1950 any British warships cruising the coast fired salvos as a mark of respect.

H.M.S. *Victoria*/H.M.S. *Camperdown*

June 22, 1893
Tripoli, Africa

The H.M.S. *Victoria* was the flagship of Britain's Mediterranean fleet, a steamship with up to 700 men aboard at the head of a line of ships. She was lost in an astonishing aberration by her commander, Vice-Admiral Sir George Tryon, and rammed by a sister ship of the fleet. Inexplicably, Tryon signaled that *Victoria* and a parallel ship H.M.S. *Camperdown* should both turn inward. They were but 1,200 yards (1,100 m.) apart when the order was given. Soon afterward the collision happened and, before going down with his ship, Tryon was heard to cry "It is entirely my fault." What possessed Tryon to cause such a tragedy nobody knows. But thanks to a manuscript left by survivor, we do know something of the last moments of the *Victoria*. Stoker James Curran gave his account of the tragedy in a personal document in which he likened the incident to the charge at Balaclava . . . He wrote:

". . . someone blundered and it is blunders such as this as makes wives widows, children orphans and cost so many British bluejackets their lives . . .

RIGHT: The *Victoria* shortly after being rammed by the *Camperdown*. When the *Camperdown* drew clear of the *Victoria*, the Admiral turned his ship's head to land with the intention of running her ashore. The water, however, poured so rapidly into the enormous breach that her bow soon began to disappear below the waves.

RIGHT: The wreck of the *Granite State,* November 4, 1895. This ship was en route from Falmouth to Swansea when she struck the Runnelstone, three miles southeast of Land's End. Rescuers managed to haul her off and she was towed to Porthcurno. However, further attempts to save her were thwarted by the cargo of wheat that she was carrying. This swelled with sea water and burst the *Granite State*'s hatches. As she settled further into the water the crew were forced to abandon ship. Sightseers were able to enjoy the scene for only a few days before the vessel was broken up by savage winter storms.

"We could hear the guns on the battery deck taking charge and rushing from port to starboard, smashing everything before them. At this juncture the order was given (to jump).

"The men sprang from the port side in scores and as the *Victoria* capsized they were smashed and killed on the vessel's rolling chocks and those that went . . . aft were cut to pieces by the propellers, which were turning with frightful speed at the time . . .

"As the vessel sank there was a terrible suction and time after time I was sucked below but again and again I came to the surface amidst hundreds of my comrades . . ."

Curran was in the water for 40 minutes before being picked up by H.M.S. *Dreadnought*. He was one of the lucky ones. More than 400 of his fellows were killed.

Aden

June 9, 1897
Sokotra, India

A P&O steamship weighing in at 2,517 tons, the *Aden* was five years old when she struck rocks off Sokotra in the early hours of the morning. Those 47 unlucky souls who left the wreck in lifeboats perished in stormy seas and it was the remaining 34 passengers and 51 crew aboard the wreck who were saved. But they had to endure terrible privations for 17 days before the Royal Indian marine steamship *Mayo* arrived on the scene to rescue them.

U.S.S. *Maine*

February 15, 1898
Havana, Cuba

The loss of the battleship U.S.S. *Maine* remains one of the most controversial events in American maritime history. After the disaster the court of inquiry, convened on the U.S.S. *Mangrove* in Havana Harbor, concluded that a submarine mine had exploded against the hull of the warship but failed to name those responsible. Crew losses were high—261 officers and men were killed and, of the 94 saved, more than half suffered injuries.

The *Maine* was anchored off Havana, Cuba, to protect U.S. nationals or evacuate them if the unrest in the Spanish colony threatened their lives. On the evening of the 15th, the battleship's commander, Captain Charles Sigsbee, was on deck, enjoying a fine cigar. So far there had been no

RIGHT: U.S.S. *Maine*, the ship which was used as an excuse to start the Spanish-American War after a mysterious explosion sent her to the bottom of Havana Harbor.

incidents, although Sigsbee, a careful officer, had posted extra guards on the ship and ordered that steam be kept up in two boilers rather than the more usual one. Satisfied that all was well, Sigsbee retired to his cabin. The time was 21.40 hours. As Sigsbee settled in his cabin, the *Maine* was rocked by a massive explosion and the vessel was plunged into darkness. Sigsbee made his way through the darkness of the ship's interior to the quarter-deck, where he ordered the ship's magazines to be flooded. Those tasked with the mission saw that water was already flooding the magazines, others reported that a fire was raging out of control in a mess amidships. The warship was also listing to port. Sigsbee made the decision to abandon ship and shortly afterward the *Maine* sank to the bottom of Havana harbor as further explosions completed the work of destruction.

Views were mixed in America, but the hawks had their day. Within 70 days, war was declared and America fought its first conflict overseas. The victory was theirs—Spain lost its last major overseas colonies in defeat.

La Bourgogne

July 4, 1898
Sable Island, Nova Scotia, Canada

Dawn was fog-bound that Independence Day as *La Bourgogne*, a 7,400 ton steamer belonging to the French line Compaigne Generale Transatlantique, groped her way toward America some 60 miles (96 km.) south of Sable Island. Blasts from her horn were the only sound to pierce the blanket of fog, which smothered the area.

Suddenly, out of the gloom came the barque *Cromartyshire*, a three-masted vessel of just 1,554 tons, en route from Dunkirk to Philadelphia with a cargo of chalk. The impossible happened. The diminuitive *Cromartyshire* holed and sank the Atlantic liner, which was five times her size. *La Bourgogne* sank swiftly, with the loss of 447 passengers and 118 crew.

After surveying the limited damaged to their own ship, crew on the *Cromartyshire* were chilled with the realization that tragedy had struck. No longer could they hear the booming foghorn, which moments before had signaled the close proximity of *La Bourgogne*. Fog lifted within 30 minutes and it was the *Cromartyshire* that rescued survivors clinging to floating debris.

RIGHT: Captain Deloncle of *La Bourgogne* who went down with nearly 600 passengers and members of his crew after a collision with the *Cromartyshire* in thick fog off Sable Island.

BELOW: *La Bourgogne,* which sank on July 4, 1898.

Mohegan

October 13, 1898
The Manacles, Cornwall, Great Britain

Lifeboatmen heroes went into action when the Atlantic Transport Line steamer *Mohegan*, en route from London to New York, was wrecked on the notorious Manacles in Cornwall, having taken a wrong turn at the Eddystone lighthouse. Darkness and stormy seas hampered the efforts of the rescuers that evening and 167 died.

Stella

March 30, 1899
The Casquets, Channel Islands, Great Britain

Stella, a 1,059 ton London and South Western Railway steamer foundered on the Casquets in the Channel Islands with the loss of 88 passengers and 24 crew. The vessel had been stricken by fog.

Cuvier

March 9, 1900
Goodwin Sands, Great Britain

The *Cuvier* was a 2,200 ton vessel designed to ply South American routes for owners Lamport & Holt of Liverpool. She became the first passenger ship of the 20th century to be lost following a collision with the *Dovre* off East Goodwin lightship. In this, the first of seven disasters to be visited on Lamport & Holt, 26 people were killed.

Saale

June 30, 1900
Hudson River, U.S.A.

The death of the *Saale* did not come as a result of sloppy seamanship, catastrophic coincidence, or freak weather. The 5,000 ton steamship was in dock in Hoboken, New Jersey, when disaster struck. A fire began in the cotton stores of Pier Three at Hoboken. Fueled by other cargo at the dockside,

RIGHT: The mass burial at St. Keverne of passengers of the *Mohegan*, October 1898. The sinking of this ship on only her second voyage remains one of the mysteries of the sea. In all, 196 were lost when the *Mohegan* struck the Manacle rocks east of the Lizard promontory at full speed on November 14, 1898, just as her passengers were sitting down to dinner. She disappeared below the waves in less than ten minutes taking with her all those who might have been able to explain the incident. The wreck is now rumored to be haunted. The few intrepid divers who have visited it report strange noises, quite unlike the normal range of sounds that can be heard under water. Other divers have experienced "shocks," similar to electrical discharges when they have touched the wreck. One diver returned to the site with a wreath for the dead and has not since experienced anything unusual.

LEFT: An aerial view of the 1901 wreck of the *Fedora* near the shore of Lake Superior in Wisconsin's Apostle Islands National Lakeshore. The capsized wreck is now a popular tourist attraction.

LEFT: The wreck of the *Reginald*. This Plymouth trawler ran aground on the coast of St. Mary's, England, in 1902.

including oil and turpentine, the blaze soon overwhelmed the pier and the ships tied to it. *Saale* was one of five ships affected. Only one escaped relatively unscathed—the rest put to sea while they were still on fire. *Saale* sank on the Jersey flats with 99 victims who had been unable to flee.

Fedora

September 20, 1901
Lake Superior

Fedora was completed in 1889 at a cost of $125,000. She bore the same name as a famous stage play of the era and was officially christened by the show's star, Fanny Davenport.

The ship, built of oak and iron, was something of a giant, with four masts, two decks, a 20 ft. (6 m.) hold, and a tonnage of 1,849.

A routine trip turned to chaos when a kerosene lamp exploded and set fire to the ship. The captain beached the blazing vessel at Chicago Beach, north of Buffalo Bay, and crew escaped in lifeboats. The following day the *Ashland Daily Press* reported the wreck "a most gruesome sight indeed." Thereafter, it became a popular excursion for sightseers.

City of Rio de Janeiro

February 22, 1902
Golden Gate Bridge, U.S.A.

A ship of the Pacific Mail Steamship Company Line, the *City of Rio de Janeiro,* was returning to America from a trip to the Far East when a calamity occurred. Reaching San Francisco in dense fog, the captain ignored warnings by a local pilot and took his ship through the Golden Gate. The ship struck rocks and the damage was sufficient to take the ship to the bottom within an hour. The captain was one of 104 people who were killed.

Camorta

April 1902
Madras, India

The *Camorta*, built in Glasgow in 1880, was a mail and passenger ship of the British India Steam Navigation Company. Her last port of call was Madras, from where she departed with 650 passengers and 89 crew.

LEFT AND BELOW LEFT: The steamship *General Slocum*, which caught fire during a pleasure cruise on New York City's East River, resulting in the loss of 1,200 lives. Many of those killed were women and children.

LEFT: A salvage team attempt to recover wreckage from the *General Slocum*.

However, she failed to reach her destination of Rangoon and it's thought that a cyclone destroyed her in the Gulf of Martaban. No survivors or wreckage were ever found.

General Slocum

June 15, 1904
East River, New York, U.S.A.

The sunday school outing promised to be a happy-go-lucky affair. Instead, disaster struck and cost the lives of 1,200 people.

It was with anticipation and excitement that the 1,800 parishioners of St. Mark's Evangelical Lutheran Church in New York, predominantly women and children, boarded the *General Slocum*. The Knickerbocker Steamship Company steamer set off down the East River for what should have been a delightful summer outing. But when a fat pan in the galley caught fire, the wooden structure of the boat was soon ablaze. Panic gripped those aboard and many were trampled to death on the decks as they sought escape.

Norge

June 28, 1904
Rockall, Scotland

Emigration to the States was still galvanizing Europe at the turn of the century. The *Norge* was just one of scores of ships who took hopefuls from Northern Europe to their destination in the New World. She left Copenhagen with 700 emigrants aboard, in addition to a crew of 80 but six days out of port she ran aground at Rockall. This left the ship stranded but unharmed—it was the captain's attempts to refloat the vessel by thrusting her into reverse that holed the underside and caused her to sink. The death toll amounted to 550.

Australia

June 29, 1904
Melbourne, Australia

P&O's *Australia* was something of a record breaker. In April 1893, six months after coming into service, she set a new world-beating time for the journey between Britain and Australia when she steamed from London to

ABOVE AND LEFT: P&O's *Australia* lies on the rocks in Melbourne following a navigational error. In this case the crew and passengers were fortunate and were able to reach the shore safely. However, the ship was too badly damaged to rescue and she was stripped bare by salvagers before fire destroyed the remaining hull.

Adelaide in just 26 days 16 hours. Yet she came to a sad end following a pilot error, which had the 6,900 ton ship run aground at Corsair Roc, Melbourne. Although the accident happened in the dead of night, all 300 people aboard were taken to safety. Her cargo and internal fittings were likewise removed and sold. Within days, the empty hulk was destroyed by fire.

Sirio

August 4, 1906
Hormigas Island, Spain

On the face of it, the chosen course seemed like a captain's mad lapse. The *Sirio*, a ship of 380 ft. (116 m.) in length and more than 4,000 tons in weight, was skirting the rocky outcrops of Hormigas Island during a voyage between Genoa in Italy and Montevideo in South America. Nor was the ship traveling cautiously—the *Sirio* hit the island's rocks at full speed. The shuddering crunch sparked panic among the 645 passengers and 127 crew and fights broke out for the safety devices aboard. The incident claimed the lives of 442 people. It was all the more shameful when a subsequent inquiry discovered the ship had been illegally involved in boarding Spanish immigrants, which was why she had been traveling so close to the land.

Prinzessin Victoria Luise

December 16, 1906
Caribbean

Arthur Ballin, director of the Hamburg American line, was one of the innovators of the holiday trade—rather than leave his ships idle in the winter, he chose to employ them on cruises. The notion, first put in practice in 1891, was a winner, and cruises became an integral feature of leisure pursuits for the wealthy.

The *Prinzessin Victoria Luise* was something of a veteran cruiser, having undertaken numerous such trips since being built in 1900. On her final, fateful voyage she had departed New York for the Caribbean and was sailing along the coast of Jamaica without a pilot when she ran onto rocks. Despite panic among the passengers, all were evacuated without loss of life, but the ship was left at the mercy of the elements. Captain H. Brunswig was mortified that a course he himself had set had ended in the loss of a magnificent craft. Ten days later he locked the door of his cabin, put a gun to his head, and pulled the trigger.

Dakota

March 7, 1907
Yokohama

The *Dakota* and her sister ship, the *Minnesota,* were the giants of the water-ways. Each weighed in excess of 20,000 tons and measured a massive 630 ft. (192 m.) in length and 74 ft. (23 m.) across the beam. Apart from her ample freight capacity, the *Dakota* also had space enough for 300 first class and 2,400 steerage passengers. She was the largest American-built passenger ship when she was commissioned in 1905 and nothing dwarfed her mighty dimensions until the *Virginia* was built and launched in 1928.

The *Dakota* came to her ignominious end after breaching on an under-water reef. Passengers and crew safely abandoned ship, but the vessel was stranded like a beached whale. Two weeks later she was smashed to pieces in a storm. The captain never took a helm again and worked as a night watchman for the rest of his days.

Neustria

November 1908
Atlantic

No one knows the fate of the *Neustria*, a ship of the French Fabre Line that weighed some 2,900 tons and had room aboard for more than 1,100 passengers. The doomed ship sailed from New York on October 27—and after leaving the safety of the harbor she was never seen again. No survivors or debris were ever found. Company officials and distraught relatives were left to speculate about what occurred to the liner and how or why she was claimed by the sea.

Republic

January 23, 1909
South of Nantucket, U.S.A.

The worth of radio aboard ship was illuminated fully for the first time in the drama that followed the collision between *Republic*, a 15,378 ton White Star liner and the *Florida*. *Republic* had 250 first class and 211 steerage passengers aboard, as well as 300 crew, as it cut a path through the waters 20 miles (32 km.) south of Nantucket. They were out of New York, bound for

the Mediterranean and in the vicinity was the Italian emigrant steamer *Florida.* Thick fog had descended before dawn and, following the same pattern of numerous accidents before and since, the two ships were unable to detect one another in time and a collision occurred, claiming three lives. The situation was grim. Still, the *Republic*'s wireless operator Jack Binns could put the new radio system through its paces. He got to work, sending out the first distress call ever made in such a manner. The recognized code he used was C.Q.D.,which would soon be replaced with S.O.S. His task was to alert other ships to the plight of the *Republic* and he succeeded with the *Baltic*, *Furnessia*, and *La Lorraine* answering his call. More than that, he guided the *Baltic* to the stricken *Republic*, which was in darkness following the collision in a black sea, without a further crash occurring. Binns sent out 200 messages that night. A tribute to his efforts is the small death toll—just four died—in what otherwise might have been a full-blown catastrophe.

Slavonia

June 10, 1909
Flores Island, Atlantic

This 10,000 ton vessel takes its place in the history books as the only Cunard ship lost at sea during peacetime. Bound for Trieste from New York and Slavonia, it was beached on Flores Island. Thanks to the wireless on board, two German steamers in the vicinity arrived on the scene to rescue passengers. She was so badly gashed by the rocks that the *Slavonia* was considered a complete loss.

Waratah

July 1909
South Atlantic

The *Waratah* is another enigma of the high seas. Still in her first year of service, she was the pride of the Blue Anchor Line, a London-based shipping company. She boasted a length of 465 ft. (142 m.) and weighed in at more than 9,300 tons. Her interior was said to resemble the London Ritz.

There were 92 passengers aboard when the *Waratah* steamed out of Durban on July 26, heading for Cape Town. The following day she signaled to the passing ship *Clan Macintyre*—*Waratah* had no radio—and then she simply vanished. Vicious weather was the prime suspect. Still, a search of the area by the British government and others failed to turn up a single piece

of wreckage. Relatives feared she was drifting helplessly in the ocean having lost all power, with the passengers reduced to eating one another to keep starvation at bay. An official inquiry in London found nothing of the sort— but was unable to say just what had occurred. In an effort to discover the truth, writer and spiritualist Sir Arthur Conan Doyle held a seance in which dead passengers allegedly related how a giant wave struck the ship and capsized it. This had some credence as the phenomena of freak waves around the Cape of Good Hope is well-known and recent research has indicated that a British soldier standing on the South African coast saw a ship overturned by a wave. The search for the wreck goes on. Among those still trying to discover what happened to the *Waratah* is author Clive Cussler. "The *Waratah* is up there with the all-time mysteries of the sea," he said. "A group of U.S. eccentrics just want the thrill of finding the ship."

Lucania

August 14, 1909
Liverpool, Great Britain

When she first sailed, she was the largest ship in the world. The *Lucania* was luxuriously appointed, which delighted her passengers, and fast, which thrilled her owners, the Cunard Line. In 1893 she won the coveted Blue Riband for achieving speeds in excess of 20 kts. across the Atlantic. The end came when she was eaten up by fire as she lay in Huskisson Dock in Liverpool. Her finery destroyed, she was deemed uneconomic for refurbishment and sold for scrap.

Orinoco

August 18, 1909
Nova Scotia, Canada

The schooner *Orinoco*, built in 1902, foundered at Sambro, Nova Scotia, with the loss of 11 lives.

BELOW: Wreck of the *Gunvor*. This three-masted steel barque was the largest ship ever lost to the rocks of Black Head, northeast of Mevagissey, which she struck in heavy fog while carrying a cargo of nitrates from South America. She was wrecked so close inshore that her fortunate crew were all able to escape by a rope ladder that was attached to her bowsprit.

La Seyne

November 14, 1909
Singapore

La Seyne is the unenvied holder of the record for the world's fastest-sinking ship. After colliding with the British India liner *Onda* in the Rheo Straits en route to Singapore, *La Seyne* hit the floor in just two minutes. Those passengers lucky enough to throw themselves from the rapidly disappearing vessel found themselves floundering in shark-infested waters. The *Onda* plucked 61 people from the sea, leaving 101 unaccounted for.

General Chanzy

February 10, 1910
Minorca, Mediterranean

After leaving Marseilles, the ill-fated *General Chanzy* was dogged by bad weather. To escape the storms, the ship's captain sought shelter in the Balearic Islands, but during that terrible night the engines failed and left the vessel helpless in the throes of the storm. Such was the power of the sea that it hurled the substantial 2,200 ton ship against the rocks, where she split and sank. Just one man out of a total of 157 on board survived.

Madalene Cooney

December 28, 1911
Cape Hatteras, U.S.A.

Nine crewmen died when the 19-year-old schooner *Madalene Cooney* collided with the steamship *Warrington* 12 miles (19 km.) north of Cape Hatteras.

Patrician

March 15, 1912
Nova Scotia, Canada

A schooner built in 1905, the *Patrician* became stranded at Jordan Bay, Nova Scotia, and 10 lives were lost.

Titanic

April 14, 1912
Atlantic

The ship was dubbed "unsinkable." But, as everybody knows, the *Titanic* went to the bottom of the Atlantic with 815 passengers and 688 crew still aboard. She departed Southampton on April 10, amid some fanfare. *Titanic*, so mighty and opulent, could only be matched at sea by her sister ship *Olympic*, which had gone into service the previous year.

After two stops, at Cherbourg and Cork, she headed out into the Atlantic with 2,206 people aboard. The *Titanic*'s 46,329 tons sliced through the calm waters, the huge turbines driving her forward at maximum speed of 22.5 kts, the passengers and crew secure in the knowledge that the liner boasted not only luxurious comforts but state-of-the-art safety measures. The liner had been fitted with a double-bottom, in the unlikely event that she might be holed. She also had 15 transverse bulkheads running the length of the vessel to isolate incoming water in case she sprang a leak. So confident were they of her safety that the White Star Line, owners of the *Titanic*, had deemed it unnecessary to carry sufficient lifeboats for all the passengers and crew, although the ship was sailing in accordance with British safety rules.

During the morning of April 14, the temperature dropped suddenly and the captain, Edward Smith, was warned by his radio operators that there were icebergs in the region. Further warnings were delivered during the day. In spite of these messages, the *Titanic* did not drop speed; there was the promised prestige of a headline-grabbing, swift passage to America, with a welcoming committee waiting in New York, to consider.

Most disastrously of all, a warning from the *Mesaba*, at 21.40 hours, that icebergs were directly in the *Titanic*'s path, was received by the wireless operator but may never have reached the bridge. Shortly before midnight the lookout shouted: "Iceberg right ahead." The bridge ordered evasive action, but it was too late. As the bow of the ship began to swing to port, an immense iceberg scraped along her starboard side below the water line. There was barely a jolt to disturb the partying passengers, or awake those in their cabins. The officers on the bridge watched the dim shape of the iceberg slip away. Captain Smith, who had been relaxing elsewhere in the ship, raced to his post. He arrived on the bridge as the first officer was ordering: "Stop engines." Smith sent below for damage reports and could hardly believe his ears when he was told that a huge rent had been torn down the side of the liner. Water was pouring in at an alarming rate—and the water-tight bulkheads, in which so much faith had been placed, were now breached. The greatest liner the world had ever seen was sinking. The

liner's passengers were blissfully unaware of the peril they were facing—so gentle had been the collision that few of them had even commented on it. Some of the more energetic wandered onto the open decks and picked up bits of ice to freshen their glasses of whisky. One group even began a "snowball" fight with debris that had been blown off the passing iceberg.

Captain Smith was a highly experienced skipper and reacted calmly to the knowledge that a death knell had been sounded for the liner with which he had been entrusted. He immediately ordered the radio room to put out distress calls and later, had the lifeboats uncovered and made ready while the passengers were raised from their slumbers by apologetic knocks on their cabin doors. Only then did he authorize distress rockets to be launched. As the bleary-eyed passengers arrived on deck, the lifeboats were swung out and the order passed down the line: "Women and children first." Now was there the first hint of panic among the passengers; but even the crew were in confusion, never having performed a full boat drill during sea trials. They failed to find many of the collapsible life rafts, which had been stowed in inaccessible places, and even when they uncovered these rafts, they did not know how to assemble them. There was milling and shouting and screaming and all the associated sounds of panic among men and women who feared that they were about to die.

Meanwhile, the radio operators had alerted two other liners to the *Titanic*'s plight. One was the *Frankfort* and the other the *Carpathia*. The captain of the latter was so incredulous at the news that the "unsinkable" *Titanic* was in trouble that he twice asked his radio operators whether they had got the message right. When assured that they had, and believing that his vessel was closest to the *Titanic*, he ordered his engine room: "Give it everything we have." The *Carpathia*, however, was 60 miles (96 km.) away. Much closer was another liner, the *California*, which was only 19 miles (30 km.) from the *Titanic*. Aboard the *California*, the *Titanic*'s distress flares had been seen by crewmen, who reported them to the bridge, but who had then been told that they must either be celebratory rockets or a false alarm. The *California* remained stationary as the *Titanic* slowly sank . . .

It was now around 02.00 hours and the bows of the *Titanic* were beginning to dip lower in the icy black North Atlantic. The lifeboats which had been filled but not lowered, in the hope of rescue, were now sent down to the calm waters below. Many were only half full. One of the ship's bands, which had been keeping spirits up playing ragtime tunes struck up the refrain "Autumn" and the haunting sound wafted across the black sea as the weeping women in the lifeboats watched their menfolk waving from the decks high above them. At 02.20 Captain Smith, having now realized that no other vessel was coming to his aid, ordered: "Abandon ship!" The *Titanic* was at an almost 90 degree angle in the ocean, her lights still twinkling and reflecting on the lifeboats drifting away from the final horror shortly to come. As if wanting to escape their inevitable fate for just a few

ABOVE: The proud and stately *Titanic* prepares for her maiden voyage.

RIGHT: Ice in the region of *Titanic*'s demise (latitude 41° 46'N and longitude 50° 14'W). The larger iceberg just left of center is believed by some to be the one which sank the *Titanic*.

RIGHT: *Titanic*'s Boat Deck. Although the ship complied with safety regulations for her time, there were far too few lifeboats to accommodate all of the passengers. There were just 20 in all—14 standard, two emergency clippers, and four collapsible. This lack was compounded by many of the boats being launched with far less than their full complement.

seconds longer, some of those who had not made it into the lifeboats scrambled up the decks like mountaineers to reach the doomed ship's stern, pointing upwards like a skyscraper. Then she went down. There was a rumble of machinery crashing from stern to bow, then a hissing and bubbling as the boilers exploded. As the *Titanic* descended through 13,000 ft. (3,961 m.) of water, a giant vortex was created, which sucked debris and bodies into the depths. Those in the water who were not dragged down by the whirlpool did not drown; they died of cold within two minutes of hitting the water. On the surface, newly-widowed women in the lifeboats wept in the bitterly cold night air. At 04.00 hours the *Carpathia* arrived and took aboard all those in the lifeboats. Only later did the final, dreadful accounting take place. Of the 2,206 passengers and crew aboard, a horrifying 1,523 were lost.

The loss of the *Titanic*, as numerous books, television programs, and movies indicate, remains the benchmark by which other disasters at sea are measured. There is no doubt that the catastrophe was caused by the collision with an iceberg, which ripped a huge, fatal gash in the liner's starboard side allowing water to pour, initially, into several holds, and subsequently filling all of the vessel's remaining watertight compartments. However, human error also played its part. Smith had received warnings of icebergs ahead from the *Caronia*, *Baltic*, and *Amerika* and still chose to sail at full speed at night. Also, evidence from Harland & Wolff, the ship's manufacturers, suggests that a bow on collision would not have led to the sinking. Changing course had inadvertently brought about the tragedy. As recently as 1998, naval architect William Garzke claimed that passengers and crew could have saved the *Titanic* from going under had they used bedding to stuff the cracks in the hull. Another theory says the construction of the rivets was to blame. The lack of lifeboats though, must surely be the most astounding failure in this catalog of disasters. Afterward, a British inquiry decided that the law must change and all ships henceforth had to carry sufficient lifeboats for everyone aboard. The public's obsession with the *Titanic* remains. The majesty of the ship was painstakingly recreated for James Cameron's Oscar-winning epic, which opened in 1997. The film cost $400 million, many times the cost of the original ship, and featured genuine footage of the wreck laying on the ocean floor 370 miles (595 km.) off Newfoundland. Such is the technology available today that cameras have been able to record the ship's cranes, portholes, cutlery, and decking, as well as hundreds of other items. There seems little prospect of a major salvage operation though, not least because the wreckage is the grave of so many.

RIGHT: The final seconds of the *Titanic* as she slips beneath the waves and begins her long plummet to the ocean floor. The courage of the crew kept all her lights blazing until just before this final moment.

RIGHT: Lifeboat number 14, with Fifth Officer Lowe in charge, approaches the *Carpathia*. In tow is a collapsible boat.

RIGHT: *Titanic* is now an eerie sight; the official grave for the 1,523 souls that died that night. Scientists suggest that the work of tiny microorganisms will soon destroy the wreck altogether.

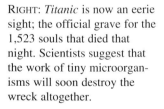

Volturno

October 1913
North Atlantic

No fewer than 10 vessels raced to the scene when they received the S.O.S. signal from the stricken *Volturno*. They were met with a sight that would haunt them forever. A blaze fueled by cargo, which included chemicals and straw goods, and fanned by a strong wind was consuming the 3,500 ton ship. The 560 terrified passengers on a passage from Rotterdam to New York were huddled on the deck awaiting rescue as the ship was tossed this way and that by high seas. Crewmen, numbering nearly 100, tried to fight the flames. Drama continued when four lifeboats were lost as they were being launched. A rescue operation was attempted but was severely hampered by the appalling conditions—when the *Volturno* finally sank the next day, the death toll stood at 136.

Edmund Fitzgerald

November 9, 1913
Lake Superior, U.S.A.

Severe storms and squalls can blow just as hard across the lakes as they can on any ocean. That November night no fewer than 18 ships and 413 lives were lost during one especially turbulent tempest which swept across the Great Lakes. The freighter *Edmund Fitzgerald*, over 700 ft. (213 m.) long and 75 ft. (23 m.) wide, was sailing from Superior Harbor, Wisconsin, loaded with some 26,000 tons of ore and 7,500 gallons of fuel. Lake Superior was calm—but not for long. The following day, winds reached 65 m.p.h. (105 k.p.h.) and huge waves battered the freighter. Captain Ernest McSorley was not unduly worried however, even when damage was caused to railing and vents, and he carried on his course for Lake Huron Locks, 100 miles (160 km.) away. Just before 17.00 hours the ship was in radio contact with the *Arthur M. Anderson*, another freighter heading for Lake Huron. After outlining the problems caused by the storm, the last transmission received was "We're holding our own." Nothing was heard from the *Edmund Fitzgerald* again. Several days later the Coast Guard located the wreck in 530 ft. (162 m.) of water. The ship had split in two with the bow section 170 ft. (52 m.) from the capsized stern section. Whatever caused her to founder must have happened very suddenly. The crew did not even have time to send out a distress signal. The investigating board concluded that a short voyage in these usually protected waters, using a

ABOVE: Grim faced survivors of the *Volturno* disaster at Liverpool on board the *Devonian*. The date of the photograph is October 10, 1913.

RIGHT: The broken prow of the lifeboat from the sunken ore carrier *Edmund Fitzgerald* on display at the S.S. Valley Camp, Sault Ste. Marie, Michigan. The ship was overwhelmed so suddenly that none of the crew had time to escape.

familiar route, could have led to, "complacency and an overly optimistic attitude." Huge ocean or Great Lake, the sea can never be taken for granted by mariners.

Empress of Ireland

May 29, 1914
Canada

She wasn't as large and luxurious as the *Titanic*, but the disaster that occurred when the *Empress of Ireland* slipped beneath the waves was every bit as shocking. A tragic 80 percent of passengers aboard—a total of 840—perished alongside 172 crew members.

The sleek *Empress of Ireland* was a 14,200 ton ship, built in 1905, which plied the Liverpool-Quebec route. The ship was no status symbol but was nevertheless fast and comfortable. She was about to enter the open sea after departing Canada when fog rolled in and calamity occurred. A Norwegian collier *Storstad* traveling toward port had spotted the lights of the *Empress* before visiblity diminished. Although both ships were aware of the other, a collision still occurred. *Storstad* gouged a hole measuring some 25 ft. (8 m.) in the liner, allowing thousands of gallons of water to pour in. Ten minutes after the impact, the *Empress* smacked onto her side and then went under. Most of the passengers were sleeping, which explains why so few were saved. The story of the *Empress* has always been overshadowed by that of the *Titanic*, which preceded it, and the First World War, which followed a month later.

Montrose

December 1914
Goodwin Sands, Great Britain

The *Montrose* is remembered not for the manner in which she sank but for the extraordinary events that took place on her decks when she was afloat.

Launched in 1897 (on the same day that Marconi sent his first true wireless message from the South Foreland lighthouse on England's southeast coast), the *Montrose* was a steel ship weighing in at 5,431 tons. She was far from luxurious, but that was fine by the emigrant farmers who made up the majority of her passengers as she traveled between Liverpool and Montreal. On July 20, 1910, she was berthed at Antwerp, preparing to sail for Quebec. At the time rumors were rife about the presence in Belgium of Dr. Hawley Harvey Crippen and his lover Ethel le Neve. Crippen was a wanted man

RIGHT: The three-masted ship *Cromdale*, battered by a southwesterly gale. The storm was so severe that it broke this Aberdeen ship into pieces within only two hours. The power of storms at sea can sometimes send a ship, its passengers, and crew, to the bottom almost without trace within minutes. Many of the ships that are lost without trace and have sent no final distress messages simply do not have the time.

RIGHT: A dramatic picture of the *Empress of Ireland*'s tragic demise. To the right of the painting can be seen the *Storstad* which collided with the *Empress of Ireland* on the night of May 29, 1914. Even though the ships were both aware of each other's presence, the fog was so thick that visibility was reduced to just a few yards and neither ship was able to detect how close they were to each other. In all, 1,012 lives were lost. At the time of the collision the 3,561 ton *Storstad* was loaded with 10,000 tons of coal. She collided directly between the twin red funnels of the *Empress* and, 14 minutes later, the passenger liner turned turtle and sank. The loss of the *Empress of Ireland* ranks as one of the worse maritime disasters of all time.

LEFT: The *Montrose* in Millwall docks, London. This famous ship is remembered for the dramatic events which took place on board. She eventually foundered on Goodwin sands, Dover, England.

FAR LEFT: The murderer, Dr. Hawley Harvey Crippen.

LEFT: Ethel le Neve, Crippen's lover, with whom he was caught on the *Montrose*, and BELOW LEFT, Crippen's murdered wife, Cora.

after the dismembered body of his wife was discovered under the cellar floor of his London home.

The captain of the *Montrose* was Henry Kendall, an observant fellow, whose suspicions were quickly aroused by one passenger, Mr. Robinson, traveling with his son. Kendall noticed that the pair were uneasy in company, that the older man had recently shaved off a moustache, and that he bore a mark on the bridge of his nose where he had once clearly worn glasses. When Kendall spotted a revolver in Robinson's pocket, he wired the Liverpool office of the Canadian Pacific. "One hundred and thirty miles west of Lizard . . . have strong suspicions that Crippen London cellar murderer and accomplice are among saloon passengers . . . Accomplice dressed as boy; voice, manner, and build undoubtedly a girl."

Inspector Dew of Scotland Yard found a faster ship, the *Laurentic*, and boarded the *Montrose* off Canada. There are two versions of what happened next. The first has Dew greeting Crippen by name and the murderer, who would be hanged within four months, responding: "Thank God it's over. The suspense has been too great." Another story circulating has Crippen cursing Kendall. This has gained some credence among superstitious seafaring folk, as Kendall was the captain of another ill-fated ship which went down close to the spot where the curse was allegedly issued.

The *Montrose* continued working the same route in obscurity until she was sold to the Admiralty in October 1914. She was to have her holds filled with cement to block Dover harbor from enemy attack but before work was finished, she broke free from her moorings, drifted onto the Goodwin Sands, and foundered. The mast of the *Montrose* remained visible until 1963, when it finally snapped and vanished.

Lusitania

May 7, 1915
Atlantic Ocean

Ships carrying the passengers of noncombatant countries run a great risk of being sunk by military action when sailing in wartime. One of the most infamous and controversial of such sinkings concerns the *Lusitania*, a former Blue Riband holder, which succumbed to a torpedo fired by German submarine *U-20*. The Cunard Line's *Lusitania*, had been operating as a passenger liner since her maiden voyage in September 1907, and continued to carry passengers during World War I, despite the fact that she had been fitted with armaments and converted into an armed auxiliary cruiser in 1913.

On May 1, 1915, the *Lusitania*, commanded by Captain William Turner, slipped her moorings in New York and headed out on her 202nd trans-

Atlantic journey, to Liverpool. On board were a crew of some 700 and more than 1,250 passengers, including 157 Americans. Also on board, stored against the bulkhead leading into the No.1 boiler room, were nearly 1,500 cases of shells and 5,000 cases of cartridges. The cruise went smoothly until the *Lusitania* closed with the coast of southern Ireland and was steaming some ten miles (16 km.) off the Old Head of Kinsale. Turner received reports of U-boat activity in the area and ordered that the ship's lifeboats be swung out ready for immediate launch, and that the ship be blacked-out. He also placed extra lookouts. Turner was wise to have taken these precautions. The *U-20*'s captain, Walter Schweiger, was under orders to sink either the *Lusitania* or the *Mauretania*. Schweiger, a ruthless and skilled commander, had already sunk three vessels before encountering the *Lusitania*. He sighted her at 13.20 hours on May 7, and was surprised at his good fortune in finding the converted liner sailing in a perfectly straight line rather than a zigzag pattern. At 14.10 Schweiger ordered the firing of a single torpedo against the *Lusitania*, which was some 700 yards (640 m.) distant. The torpedo struck home, exploding against the hull of the *Lusitania* next to the bulkhead where the cases of ammunition were stored. A second detonation followed—that of the explosives. *Lusitania* was mortally wounded and took on a fifteen-degree list. The passengers showed remarkable calm. However, the list to starboard rendered the ship's port lifeboats inoperable and people began to crowd to the starboard side where there were lifeboats that could be filled and lowered to relative safety. It was soon found though, that there were far to few lifeboats available—and too little time left for the number of passengers on board.

Commader Schweiger, on his way home to Wilhelmshaven, wrote the following account of the sinking in his log.

"3.10 pm: Torpedo shot at distance of 700 meters, running three meters below the surface. Hits steering center below bridge. Unusually great detonation with large cloud of smoke and debris shot above the funnels. In addition to torpedo a second explosion must have taken place (boiler, coal or powder?). Bridge and part of the ship where the torpedo hit are torn apart and fire follows.

"The ship stops and very quickly leans to starboard, at the same time sinking at the bow. It looks as though it would capsize in a short time. There is great confusion on board. Boats are cleared and many of them lowered into the water. Many boats fully loaded drop down into the water bow or stern first and capsize. I could not have fired a second torpedo into this throng of humanity attempting to save themselves. The boats on the port side cannot be made clear because of the slanting position. At the front of the ship the name *Lusitania* in gold letters can be seen. The funnels are painted black. The stern flag is not hoisted."

TOP: A compelling picture of the *Lusitania*, by Charles Dixon, as she sinks. The loss of the *Lusitania*, although within the rules of war, greatly outraged senior figures in the U.S. government as well as many ordinary citizens. Although the United States did not join World War I until 1917, the torpedoing of the liner did much to turn U.S. public opinion against Germany.

ABOVE: A life jacket from the *Lusitania* that was found in the Delaware five years after the ship sank.

RIGHT: Captain Turner, commander of the *Lusitania*.

The *Lusitania* sank some 20 minutes after being hit by the torpedo. She went down with most of her crew and passengers, and only 663 people were saved, many of which were crew. Among the passengers lost were 124 U.S. citizens, including the multimillionaire Alfred Vanderbilt. Those who survived included Captain Turner, a woman who floated to shore in an armchair, and a mother who prematurely gave birth in the water, along with her child. Passenger Mrs. Joan Murray also made it back to shore. She was also a survivor of the *Titanic* disaster and escaped with her life once more in 1927 when the *Celtic* collided with the *Anaconda* in the Atlantic.

The loss of the *Lusitania*, although within the rules of war, greatly outraged senior figures in the U.S. government and many ordinary citizens. In America, Judge Julius M. Mayer ruled: "The cause of the *Lusitania* sinking was the illegal act of the Imperial German government, through its instrument, the submarine commander." Although the United States did not join World War I until 1917, the torpedoing of the liner did much to turn U.S. public opinion against Germany.

The policy that had *Lusitania* sailing in unguarded seas which the Germans had declared a war zone, has since come under scrutiny. There's speculation that Winston Churchill's comment made in 1914, alluding to the ship being "45,000 tons of live bait," might be close to the mark.

RIGHT: Mr. J. Ayala, the Cuban Consul, was a survivor of the *Lusitania*. This picture was taken soon after the remaining passengers and crew were brought to shore at Queenstown, Ireland.

RIGHT: *Lusitania* survivors, Queenstown, Ireland.

Eastland

July 24, 1915
Chicago River, U.S.A.

When the steamship *Eastland* capsized in the Chicago River that summer's day, 812 people lost their lives.

Marowijne

August 1915
Gulf of Mexico

Marowijne is one of the few ships to fall into the "lost without trace" category. Owned by the United Fruit Company of New York, she sailed from Belize, British Honduras, with 40 first class passengers, crew, and 40,000 bunches of bananas. Nothing is known of her fate after that but it is assumed she fell victim to the hurricane that was causing difficulties in the Gulf of Mexico at the time. Only one item was ever recovered—a single life preserver.

VON TIRPITZ

LUSITANIA

Queenstown, 7. Mai 1915.
Der Cunardbampfer „Lusitania" ist torpediert worden und gesunken.

Ancona

November 8, 1915
Atlantic

An innocent victim of World War I hostilities, the *Ancona* was two days out of Naples, heading to New York, when she was torpedoed. The 8,885 ton steamer quickly took on water after she was holed. Of the 446 people aboard, only 252 survived, after the French cruiser *Pluton* arrived on the scene. The rogue submarine that caused the tragedy was flying an Austrian flag but was in fact the German *U-38*. The incident occurred long before Italy, or indeed America, had joined the Allied effort against Germany.

Mont Blanc

December 30, 1917
Halifax, Nova Scotia, Canada

By any standards, the devastation of the French freighter *Mont Blanc* by a sudden explosion must rank as one of the greatest shipping disasters of all types. Not only was the ship obliterated, but the Canadian port of Halifax was also devastated.

The incident took place at the height of World War I as the *Mont Blanc*, packed with high explosives destined for Europe, sailed into Halifax, Nova Scotia, where it was to rendezvous with H.M.S. *High Flyer*, a cruiser, and other merchantmen for the crossing of the Atlantic. The *Mont Blanc* reached Halifax at about 09.00 hours on December 6. Halifax is sited on a long, thin natural harbor that narrows to less than 800 yards (732 m.) at its entrance. As the *Mont Blanc* closed on this narrow entrance, her captain, crew, and a local pilot spotted a Belgian freighter, the *Imo*, steaming toward them. Under standing regulations, the *Imo* was supposed to pass to the starboard of the *Mont Blanc*, but its captain signaled that he was intending to pass to port. The master of *Mont Blanc* swung his rudder to port in a desperate evasive maneuver, but it was to no avail. The *Imo* crashed into the *Mont Blanc*. The point of impact coincided with the hold where highly volatile picric acid was stored.

The *Imo* was able to back away from the wreckage after the collision, but the *Mont Blanc* was dead in the water. Soon engulfed by flames, she was abandoned by her crew, who headed for shore. The freighter drifted helplessly, ever closer to the shore and the small town of Halifax. To make matters worse, another merchantman, the British *Pictou*, was at anchor alongside the harbor's Pier Eight and she too, was packed with munitions bound

for Europe. The *Pictou*'s crew, seeing the approaching danger, also abandoned ship. The crew of the cruiser, the *High Flyer*, were made of sterner stuff, and attempted to board the blazing *Mont Blanc*. Their efforts were to no avail however. Some 15 minutes after the original collision, the *Mont Blanc*'s deadly cargo exploded with truly catastrophic affect.

Some 50 percent of Halifax was destroyed by the shock waves generated by the original blast or the fires that followed. Virtually all of the dockyard buildings and loading facilities were smashed and several hundred of the dockers killed. Fires took hold among the town's wooden buildings and an estimated 25,000 people were left homeless at the height of the Canadian winter. Matters could have been made much worse if the *Pictou*, which had escaped the initial blast, had been consumed in the subsequent blaze. However, one brave man hurried on board the freighter, opened its sea-cocks, and scuttled the vessel. Nevertheless, some 3,000 people had died in the disaster and a further 7,500 were injured.

City of Athens

May 1, 1918
Atlantic City, New Jersey, U.S.A.

The 3,648 ton steamship *City of Athens* was sent to the bottom with the loss of 66 lives after a collision with the French cruiser *La Glorie* off Atlantic City.

Afrique

January 13, 1920
La Rochelle, France

The loss of the British-built but French-owned *Afrique* in 1920 remains one of the worst disasters to befall the French maritime fleet. The *Afrique*, a single-funneled steamship with a pair of auxiliary masts, was used to ferry passengers and cargoes between France and French colonies in West Africa.

Her final voyage to Dakar began in Bordeaux in January. On board the ship were over 120 crew members and 458 passengers. The master of the ship was Captain Le Du. *Afrique* got into difficulties as she was sailing through the Bay of Biscay when the vessel lost engine power and was buffeted by strong winds and high seas. Without power to maneuver, she began to drift toward the Roche-Bonne reefs, some 50 miles (80 km.) off La Rochelle. Captain Le Du ordered that a distress message be sent, and this was duly answered by the *Ceylan*, a ship owned by the same company as the *Afrique*.

However, the *Ceylan* arrived too late. *Afrique* had struck the reefs and was being battered to destruction. Two other vessels, the *Lapland* and *Anversville*, arrived to offer their assistance, but little could be done by any of the ships. A couple of lifeboats did manage to escape from the mortally wounded *Afrique*, but the fate of those remaining onboard was sealed. At 03.00 hours on the 13th, the vessel sank. The only survivors were the 32 people who had escaped on the pair of lifeboats.

Hong Koh

March 18, 1921
Swatow Harbor, China

One of the strangest sinkings in maritime history caused the loss of more than 1,000 lives. The steamer *Hong Koh*, captained by British officer Harry Holmes, was making a routine call to the ports of Swatow and Amoy in China. The voyage, however, was to be anything but routine.

The inhabitants of Amoy and Swatow had long harbored deep-seated animosity for one another. Fierce fistfights and arguments had already broken out among the passengers, who were almost exclusively from the two cities, as the *Hong Koh* approached its first port of call, Swatow. Tragically, as it turned out, an unexpectedly low tide that day made it impossible for the *Hong Koh*, which drew 22 ft. (7 m.), to pass over a sandbar that stood sentinel at the entrance to Swatow harbor.

When Captain Holmes announced this to the passengers, adding that the ship would continue to Amoy, the fighting broke out again with a new intensity. In a bid to quell the riot Captain Holmes positioned his crew in the bows of the ship, armed with hot water hoses and guns. No one seemed to notice amidst the fury that the ship was drifting dangerously close to a razor sharp reef. As Captain Holmes and his crew prepared to fire over the rioters' heads, a bone-shaking shudder rocked the ship. She had come to grief against the rocks, tearing a huge gash in her side. Rather than quell the fighting, this seemed to refuel the hatred of the warring Chinese, and they began battling for a place in the lifeboats with knives, hatchets, axes, and anything else they could lay their hands on. Hundreds were murdered and the decks swam with blood as the sea came up to wash them clean. In the mad scramble, most of the lifeboats were either smashed against the side of the ship or overturned by the deseprate numbers trying to fight their way on board. The crew, who managed to secure a lifeboat for themselves, were part of the mere handful of survivors. Captain Holmes went to the bottom of the China Sea with his ship.

Egypt

May 20, 1922
Off France

RIGHT: The *Egypt*. This photo-graph was taken in 1897, 25 years before the *Seine* holed her and sent her to the bottom. A fortune in bullion remains on the wreck.

When *Egypt* set off from Tilbury dock in England, she had 294 crew and 44 passengers on the decks and one million pounds worth of gold and silver bars and coins stashed below. Captain Andrew Collyer was in charge of the 85 European officers aboard as well as the 208 Lascars and Genoese.

Tragedy struck 25 miles (40 km.) southwest of Ushant when dense fog rolled over the French coastline and its surrounding waters, reducing visibility drastically. The port side of *Egypt* was rammed by the French cargo steamer *Seine*. Although the freight ship was only a fifth of the size of the *Egypt*, it was equipped with heavy-duty ice-breaking bows.

During the 20 minutes it took for the *Egypt* to sink there was panic—and heroism. Ship's private, George Jenner, handed his lifebelt to a woman passenger with the words: "Here you are, madam, this belt is yours. I don't know how to swim but I'll take my chance with the others." In all, 87 people died, the survivors scrambling aboard the *Seine*.

RIGHT: The wreck of the *Dresden* which was beached after hitting rocks in 1934. Four women died when their lifeboat was caught in a propeller.

Principessa Mafalda

October 25, 1927
Brazil

Problems began for the Italian-owned *Principessa Mafalda* when a pro-peller shaft broke as she approached an island off the Brazilian coast. Water poured into the boiler room and a series of explosions followed. Mayday messages brought seven other vessels to the scene but their efforts could not save all 1,259 people aboard. When the ship capsized some four hours later, only 956 had made it to safety and more than 300 were lost.

Vestris

November 12, 1928
Atlantic

Half the passengers on the *Vestris* died when the liner went down off the coast of Virginia in heavy weather mid-way through an evacuation. The ill-fated ship capsized as the lifeboats were being filled. Apart from the 68 passengers who died, 44 crew also went down with the ship.

Celtic

December 10, 1928
Atlantic

Drama continued for 25 survivors of the *Vestris* when the *Celtic*, which was carrying them to Queenstown, was holed on rocks in gale-force winds. Their luck continued, however, as they were safely ferried to shore by the boat's tenders along with the original 224 passengers.

Dresden

June 20, 1934
North Sea

The *Dresden* had been chartered by almost 1,000 German Nazis for a North Sea cruise when it hit a submerged rock and was beached. Panic-stricken passengers plunged into the water and four women died when their lifeboat was chewed up by the ship's exposed propeller.

Morro Castle

September 8, 1934
Asbury Park, New Jersey, U.S.A.

The *Morro Castle* drew attention to shortcomings in sea-faring safety measures in a similar, spectacular style to the *Titanic*. Disabled by a blaze, 137 lives were lost on the liner as it headed for New York from Cuba with American holidaymakers aboard. Afterward an inquiry heard how panic gripped the passengers; how fire hydrants had previously been removed from the deck where the fire broke out; that the crew was incompetent; that eight life-boats were out of action and that at no time were the passengers or crew subjected to a practice drill on the voyage. Legislation was passed following the disaster to ensure that ships were better built and more professionally crewed.

RIGHT: A tiny lifeboat carrying survivors from the blazing *Morro Castle* can just be seen at the bottom of the photograph. They were fortunate: incompetence and negligence added many to the final death toll of 137.

RIGHT: The *Morro Castle* beached in the sands off Ashbury Park, New Jersey. Sightseers flocked to the wreck before it was eventually salvaged.

LEFT: Disaster strikes the French liner *L'Atlantique* near the English Channel in 1935. This unusually graphic aerial view shows smoke billowing from the ship as fire rages out of control on board.

ABOVE RIGHT: A raging fire took only one hour to wreck a Danish freighter. Loaded with nitrate, the ship caught fire at Boston, Massachusetts, and the blazing vessel was rocked with terrific explosions as firemen tried vainly to check the flames. The firefloat proves of little use in saving the ship.

BELOW RIGHT: The *Spaarndam*, a steamer of the Holland Amerika Line, which was sunk in the Thames estuary by a magnetic mine. Five people were killed.

BELOW: November 9, 1936. The broken hulk of the American steamship *Bessemer City* is battered by the waves off the coast of St. Ives, Cornwall.

LEFT: September 3, 1939. An injured survivor from the passenger ship *Athenia* is lifted to safety. The *Athenia* was torpedoed by a German U-Boat without warning off the coast of Scotland and Ireland.

BELOW: The sinking *Dunbar Castle*, January 15, 1940.

Ausonia

October 18, 1935
Alexandria, Egypt

The sleek-lined *Ausonia* was plying the triangular passenger route between Genoa, Alexandria, and Venice. On October 18, with 35 passengers and 240 crew on board, she arrived at Alexandria harbor from Haifa. Some 45 minutes after arriving, the vessel was rocked by an explosion in her boiler room, which caused a fire that swept through the ship. The passengers and crew were lucky. Alexandria was the home of the Royal Navy Mediterranean Fleet, and sailors from many warships rushed to help the stricken vessel. Thanks to their efforts, only three people on the *Ausonia* were killed, but the vessel herself was a total loss. She was towed to Trieste and broken up the following year.

Lafayette

May 4, 1938
France

As ships go, *Lafayette* had checkered history. The catalog of disasters began in 1933, when she was just three years old. A blaze engulfed the cold storage room, of all places, while she was undergoing repairs. Two years later, she was rammed by a tug; a year after that, she was in a collision with a freighter on the St. Lawrence River. Another fire caused damage when she was in for repairs in October 1936. Just 18 months later the third fire, which occurred in dry dock at Le Havre, proved to be the liner's undoing. Although her crew escaped, the ship was entirely destroyed.

Athenia

September 3, 1939
Atlantic

In an echo of the loss of the *Lusitania*, another passenger ship, the *Athenia* was sunk by a German submarine, the *U-30*, on September 3, 1939, the day Britain and France declared war on Nazi Germany following Hitler's invasion of Poland. The *Athenia* was sailing from Glasgow, via Liverpool and Belfast, for New York. It was sighted by the U-boat's captain, when it was some 250 miles (400 km.) off the coast of Northern Ireland, and at 16.00

hours two torpedoes struck the ship. On board the *Athenia* were 1,418 passengers, including over 300 U.S. citizens. The ship went down in less than 30 minutes, along with 112 of those on board.

The *Lusitania* and *Athenia* are by no means the only civilian vessels to be sunk by deliberate action. Just a few months later, on November 8, 1915, an Italian passenger liner, the *Ancona*, also fell victim to a torpedo. This time there was absolutely no justification as, at the time, Italy was a neutral country. The *Ancona* sailed from Naples on November 6, heading across the Atlantic and bound for New York. On November 8, the liner was spotted by a German submarine, which was flying under the Austrian flag. The submarine commander shadowed the liner and at about 13.00 hours fired a torpedo. The resulting explosion sealed the fate of the vessel and, despite the presence of a French warship, the *Pluton*, the loss of life was high. There were 446 people onboard the *Ancona*, of these only 194 were rescued before the ship slid beneath the waves.

Politician

1941
Off Erisksay, Scotland

Over 50 years after the *Politician* was wrecked off the Isle of Eriskay, bottles of whisky were still being discovered, having been looted by locals and then squirreled away. The *Politician* was heading for Jamaica via New Orleans with a cargo of 260,000 bottles of whisky when she sank in the Hebrides. The authorities attempted to recover the cargo but were hampered in their efforts by otherwise law-abiding local people who were astonished at their good fortune when bottles came up by the hundred on the local beach. At the time there were 40 arrests and 15 people were jailed. The incident was immortalized by Sir Compton Mackenzie in his novel *Whisky Galore*, which was later made into a film.

Grand Camp

April 16, 1947
Texas

Texas City on the United States-Gulf of Mexico coast, suffered a body blow through a ship's explosion. A freighter, the *Grand Camp*, was carrying a volatile cargo of ammonium nitrate when a fire broke out while it was at anchor. The ammonium nitrate was soon ablaze and then exploded, sending flaming debris high into the sky above the harbor. To make matters worse,

ABOVE: The Swedish ship *C.A. Banck* ran aground on the night of March 1, 1949, in heavy seas near Bloemendaal, off the Dutch Coast. The crew were all rescued by the Landvoort lifeboat.

RIGHT: This unidentified vessel caught fire off the Cape of Good Hope, South Africa in 1950.

ABOVE: The British Railways ferry steamer, the *Duke of York*, carrying 440 passengers was on a normal service run from the Hook of Holland to Harwich when it collided with the U.S. Department of Commerce ship *Haiti Victory* about 46 miles (75 km.) from Harwich. Nearby boats raced to the scene and, with 11 minesweepers which immediately left from the British port, rescued all passengers and eventually towed in the *Duke of York* which was originally reported to be sinking.

LEFT: The 20,000 ton liner *Empress of Canada* was swept by fire in Gladstone Dock, Liverpool, England, in January, 1953. This picture shows the ship, which had turned on its side, being hauled upright. The salvage operation cost £380,000.

some 50 oil tankers were loading and unloading at the time of the explosion. These tankers began to catch fire, sending thick, acrid clouds of smoke into the sky. A nearby chemical plant also went up in flames, adding to the conflagration. The local emergency services were swamped by the sheer enormity of the inferno and the fires raged virtually unchecked, destroying or damaging over 80 percent of Texas City's buildings. Estimates of the number of dead were difficult to compile but two days after the initial explosion of the *Grand Camp*, officials had reached a total of 800.

Princess Victoria

January 31, 1953
Irish Sea

Mountainous seas whipped up by winter storms sank the 2,694 ton British Rail car ferry *Princess Victoria* as it left the shelter of Stranraer harbor and entered the Irish Sea. Water forced its way through doors that were not properly secured and its cargo is thought to have shifted, flipping the ferry onto its side. There were 127 passengers aboard, including Northern Ireland M.P.s Major John Sutcliffe and Sir Walter Smiles, as well as 49 crew. Only a total of 44 survived. Among the dead was the captain, James Ferguson, who was last seen saluting as the 308 ft. (94 m.) ferry dipped beneath the waves. At an inquest, crew member Thomas McQuiston told how watertight doors were not closed even when the ferry got underway. "The water swept into the car deck and swept the cargo onto the starboard side, causing the ship to list. No attempt was or could be made to pump the water out."

Although Navy destroyer H.M.S. *Rothesay* raced to the scene, the stricken ferry had drifted from its reported position. Lifeboatmen, who faced dreadful conditions, were hailed as heroes for their attempts at a rescue.

Andrea Doria

July 25, 1956
Nantucket, Massachusetts, U.S.A.

One of the most publicized collisions of the 20th century was the one which resulted in the sinking of the *Andrea Doria*. World War II was still fresh in many people's minds and the world was only just recovering from its repercussions. Many were looking to a bright new future of technological achievement, and the loss of this passenger liner came as a hard blow. Great

ABOVE: The *Princess Victoria* founders in heavy seas.

RIGHT: The aftermath of the *Princess Victoria* disaster. Anxious onlookers watch as the injured are brought ashore from a Royal Navy destroyer which went to her aid.

hopes were invested in the sleek, luxury passenger liner *Andrea Doria*, both by its owners, Italia-Societa per Azioni di Navigazione, as well as the flagging Italian maritime fleet and she was launched with much ceremony in the early 1950s. Built by Ansaldo of Sestri, near Genoa, the 690 ft. (210 m.) long *Andrea Doria* was lavishly appointed and had sufficient cabins to carry 218 passengers in first-class accommodation, 320 in cabin class, and 703 in tourist class. The ship boasted three swimming pools and more than 30 separate public rooms. The flagship of the Italian Line, she was built to cash in on the passenger routes between Europe and North America; from her home port, Genoa, she stopped at Cannes, Naples, and Gibraltar before sailing across the North Atlantic for New York.

The *Andrea Doria*'s final voyage began when she sailed out of Genoa on her 51st trans-Atlantic voyage on July 17, 1956. The liner, commanded by Captain Peiro Calamai, was due to dock in New York on the 26th; on board were a crew of more than 500 and, after departing Gibraltar, almost 1,150 passengers. Calamai's route for the trans-Atlantic crossing would take him a little way to the south of the Nantucket Light Vessel. On July 25, the *Andrea Doria* was running at her top speed (22 kts.) as she approached to within 150 miles (241 km.) of the Light Vessel. Fog, not unusual for the time of the year, was encountered and Calamai ordered a slight reduction of speed, closed the liner's watertight doors, ordered lookouts to be posted, and turned on the *Andrea Doria*'s foghorn. As a further precaution, the vessel's navigational radar was switched on. Calamai was, like many captains of fast passenger liners, under pressure to keep to the scheduled timetable crossing but he should, by the letter of maritime procedure, have reduced his speed by more than the one knot that he ordered, particularly when the fog thickened.

At about 22.20 hours, those on the bridge of the *Andrea Doria* heard the foghorn of the Nantucket Light Vessel booming out to them from a distance of about 900 yards (820 m.). Ocean currents had pushed the *Andrea Doria* much closer to the light vessel than had been intended. Then, at around 22.40 hours, an echo on the liner's radar screen indicated a vessel almost dead ahead, steaming toward the *Andrea Doria* at approximately 18 kts. It was the Swedish-American Line's *Stockholm*, commanded by Captain Gunnar Nordensen. She had left New York harbor's pier at 57th Street at 11.30 hours on the morning of the 25th. The two vessels closed at a combined speed of almost 40 kts. Calamai, checking the *Stockholm*'s position on the radar screen at 22.45 hours, ordered a four-degree turn to port, believing that the alteration would allow the ships to pass starboard to starboard. However, maritime regulations stated that ships steaming toward each other should steer to starboard, unless there was sufficient time and distance between them. With the ships closing at nearly 40 kts, Calamai had just three to five minutes to carry out his maneuver. It was far too little time to break with accepted procedures.

RIGHT: Having been abandoned by her passengers and crew, the crippled Italian passenger ship *Andrea Doria* lists sharply to her starboard side. The liner collided with the Swedish ship *Stockholm* in thick fog off Nantucket Island.

RIGHT: A dramatic photograph as the great luxury liner *Andrea Doria* rolls onto her side seconds before plunging to the bottom of the Atlantic. More than 1,700 passengers and crew were rescued.

RIGHT: One of the *Andrea Doria* survivors arrives in New York after being rescued by the *Stockholm*.

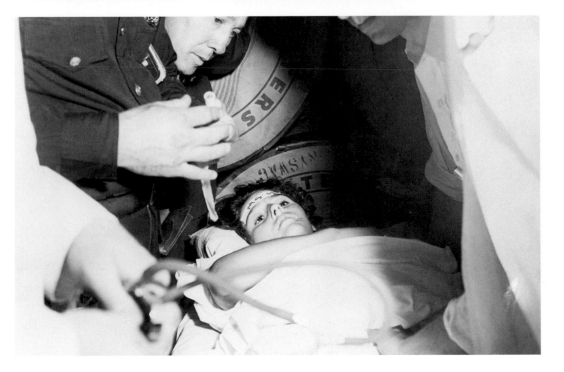

Suddenly, out of the fog, those on the *Andrea Doria*'s bridge saw lights approaching fast. Calamai ordered "hard-a-port," but it was far too late. The *Stockholm*, fitted with a strengthened bow ploughed into the *Andrea Doria*'s starboard side abreast of the bridge. There was no order to stop engines on the *Doria* in the moments immediately after the collision, which opened up the liner's side from her upper decks to her double bottom. It was now 11.10 hours. The motion of the two vessels allowed the *Stockholm* to break free, but she had some 60 ft. (18 m.) of her bow pushed back. In spite of the damage, the *Stockholm*'s forward bulkhead had held and their was no danger of sinking. In stark contrast, the *Andrea Doria*'s wounds were terminal—the liner had taken on an 18 degree list to starboard. Here, the vessel's empty fuel tanks had been ruptured in the collision and filled rapidly with sea water. The *Andrea Doria* had been built to cope with lists of up to 15 degrees and only the lifeboats on the starboard side could now be swung out. These could carry no more than half of the passengers and crew. Assistance was needed—and fast. Several vessels heeded the distress signals and first on the scene, but with only two lifeboats, was the *Cape Ann*. Other nearby vessels rushed to the scene, including the French liner *Ile de France*, which arrived at 02.00 hours on the 26th. With the liner's additional lifeboats, the safe evacuation of 1,662 passengers and crew was completed by 04.00 hours. The *Ile de France* took on board the most survivors (753) of all the rescue ships on site. However, 44 people from the *Andrea Doria* had died, as well as three on the *Stockholm*. The *Andrea Doria* was finally abandoned by a skeleton crew of volunteers at 05.30, by which time the liner was listing a crippling 40 degrees to starboard; one of the last to leave was Calamai. All of the rescue ships sailed back to New York and one of the last vessels to leave, the U.S. Coast Guard cutter *Evergreen* noted that the *Andrea Doria* sank at 10.09 hours, coming to rest in 225 ft. (70 m.) of water. The short career of the *Andrea Doria*, the first passenger liner to be built in Italy after World War II, was over. Her sinking was the first major peacetime loss of a passenger liner since the *Titanic* tragedy of 1912.

Hans Hedtoft

January 30, 1959
Atlantic

The loss of the *Hans Hedtoft*, owned by the Royal Greenland Trading Company, on January 30, 1939, plunged the Danish people into a period of national mourning. Despite the vessel's safety features, including a reinforced bow, double bottom, and numerous watertight compartments, the *Hans Hedtoft* proved to be no match for the natural elements.

On January 29, the *Hans Hedtoft* was on her maiden voyage, preparing to complete her return journey to Copenhagen from Greenland. The vessel, loaded with 55 passengers and a crew 40-strong, cast off from Godthaab from where she sailed into truly monstrous weather—gale-force winds, waves rising to 20 ft. (6 m.), and snowstorms. Visibility dropped dramatically, but the ship plowed on at around 12 kts. Disaster struck at about 11.55 hours on the following day at a point some 35 miles (56 km.) south of Cape Farewell, the most southerly point of Greenland. The vessel struck an iceberg, not seen before it was too late due to the terrible conditions. The *Hans Hedtoft*'s master, Captain P.L. Rasmussen, was able to send out a distress signal, which was picked up by two vessels, a U.S. Coast Guard ship, the *Campbell*, and the *Johanna Kruess*, a German trawler. The last message from the sinking vessel was transmitted at 15.35 hours. Both of these vessels set course for the last known position of the Danish ship, with the *Johanna Kruess* being the first to arrive on the scene at around 18.30 hours. Despite searching the area carefully, the German trawler found absolutely nothing to indicate that the *Hans Hedtoft* had ever existed. Ship, passengers, and crew had vanished. Extensive searches involving Danish maritime patrol craft and several vessels were made, but they found nothing. Bowing to the inevitable, the search was called off on February 7.

Like the *Titanic,* the *Hans Hedtoft* had collided with an iceberg on her maiden voyage, but this time there were no survivors to tell of her final minutes or the cause of the disaster.

Dara

April 9, 1961
Persian Gulf

The *Dara* operated between the Persian Gulf and India. On April 7, the ship was anchored off Dubai, picking up cargo and passengers when a severe gale blew in. The ship's captain, believing that the *Dara* could ride out the storm in open waters, sailed out of the harbor. By about 04.00 hours on April 8, he decided that the weather was subsiding and the vessel could return to Dubai to finish loading cargo and passengers. The ship never docked. At about 04.45, a large explosion had rocked the vessel and fires rapidly began to blaze. Unfortunately for those on the *Dara*, the ship's radio was out of action, so no distress call could be sent. However, one vessel, the *Empire Guillemot*, saw the disaster and rushed to help, along with three other vessels. Many of the *Dara*'s lifeboats could not be used because of the flames licking around them and many of the by-now panicking passengers rushed to the port side, where operable lifeboats were to be found. Others

ABOVE: The *Dara* steams out into the open ocean in peaceful weather. This cheerful photograph is in stark contrast to those right and below which show the shocking effects of the explosion which ripped through her in the early hours of April 9, 1961.

LEFT: The blazing *Dara*. A wall of flame blocked access to the lifeboats, many of which can still be seen on the ship.

LEFT: On board the fire ravaged *Dara* smoke still billows from the holds. This photograph was taken soon before she sank.

leapt for their lives. When a headcount was taken it was found that 584 people had been saved, although three later died through their injuries. However, 238 of those on board died due to the immediate affects of explosion and fire. The *Dara* later sank, and six months after the explosion, divers went down to the wreck which was lying in 60 ft. (18 m.) feet of water. They discovered that an explosive charge, a terrorist attack, was the likely cause of the initial explosion, although the culprits were never identified.

Save

July 8, 1961
Africa

The snub-featured *Save* was plying the ports of Mozambique when a storm blew up, engulfing the 2,039 ton ship. Although anchored at the mouth of a river, she still found herself at the mercy of the elements when the mooring broke free and a fire ignited. After being grounded for a second time, a series of explosions rocked the boat, destroying the *Save* and killing 243 passengers and 16 crew.

Venezuela

March 17, 1962
France

Was the *Venezuela* a victim of an elaborate robbery which went badly wrong? On the face of it high winds appeared to be the cause of the disaster, driving the 18,769 ton ship onto the rocks close to Cannes. Captain Michele Petro beached the ship and his crew saved the lives of the 510 passengers aboard. However, Italian police had been warned about a planned robbery to relieve the ship of its cargo of gold ingots worth $2,863,000. Further credence was added to this when it was discovered the radar aboard appeared to have been sabotaged. The gold remained safely in the holds until it was removed with official blessing.

Yarmouth Castle

November 13, 1965
Caribbean

Once again, sloppy seamanship shone through when the *Yarmouth Castle* was in jeopardy. Few of the sailors aboard had any idea about basic safety procedures, which would have enabled the safe evacuation of passengers after a fire broke out. In fact, the first lifeboat to reach a waiting freight ship was occupied by the captain, two senior officers, the bosun, and just a few passengers. In the end, the two rescue ships that responded to an S.O.S. dispatched by *Yarmouth Castle* retrieved 458 people, many of who were in the water. By the time the ship rolled over, 97 people had died.

Heraklion

December 12, 1966
Greece

The *Heraklion* began life as the *Leicestershire*, under which name the ship sailed for the Bibby Line between Britain and Burma. In 1964, the ship was sold to Greece's Typaldos Lines, refitted to carry 300 passengers as well as trucks, coaches, and cars, renamed, and put into service on the inter-island routes between Piraeus on the mainland and Heraklion on Crete.

The *Heraklion*'s final voyage began on December 7, 1966, when the vessel sailed from Crete bound for the mainland. As the *Heraklion* headed out into the Aegean, the ship was buffeted by waves whipped up by gale-force winds. The ship should have been able to withstand the rolling motion set up by the seas and wind, but matters were made much worse because loading and securing procedures had not been followed to the letter. A number of vehicles in the hold broke loose and began to career across the deck. Eventually, one substantial vehicle, a refrigerated lorry, crashed into the vessel's bow doors, forcing them open. The crew struggled to seal the opening, but to no avail, and water began to swamp the hold. The *Heraklion* took on a dangerous quantity of water and at about 02.00 hours on December 8, the ferry transmitted a distress signal. It was far too late. Several rescue vessels hurried to the spot, close to the small island of Falconara in the Cyclades, where the *Heraklion* was in difficulty. The first arrived just 30 minutes after the original distress call had been heard, yet there was no sign of the *Heraklion*. Debris from the ferry, including distinctive orange life jackets was spotted, but seemingly no survivors. In fact 47 people were later found clinging to the rocks of Falconara, but of the remainder of the 288

passengers and the crew there was no sign. The owner and general manager of the Typaldos Lines were given prison sentences in 1968.

Torrey Canyon

March 1967
Scilly Isles, Great Britain

The master of the *Torrey Canyon* was asleep in his cabin as his chief officer first picked up a radar reflection of land at 06.30 hours on the morning of March 18, 1967.

The *Torrey Canyon*, at 118,285 tons, was at that time the 13th largest vessel afloat. Nearly 1,000 ft. (300 m.) long and with a 50 ft. (15 m.) draught, she was heading for Milford Haven, South Wales, with a cargo of 120,000 tons of crude oil from Kuwait. She was owned by the Barracuda Tanker Company of Bermuda, a subsidiary of Union Oil, Los Angeles, and flew a Liberian flag. The ship was on charter to British Petroleum with a mainly Italian crew. Captain Rugiati was very experienced but he was also under some pressure to make port. The ship's agents in Milford Haven had advised him that unless he could catch the evening tide on the 18th he would have to wait until the 24th to dock—an expensive six days spent idle. The radar contact showed that the *Torrey Canyon* was heading for the gap between the Scilly Isles and Cornwall—a treacherous channel for vessels much smaller than the *Torrey Canyon*—and consequently the first officer had altered course to pass west of the islands. However, woken from his slumbers to be informed of the predicament, Captain Rugiati countermanded the order, putting the vessel back onto her previous heading. Even more baffling, he also engaged the ship's automatic pilot. The light ship guarding the Seven Stones spotted the *Torrey Canyon* and fired off warning rockets, but by the time anyone on board the supertanker became aware of the terrible danger, it was too late. At 09.15 hours the *Torrey Canyon* struck Pollard Rock, the most westerly of the Seven Stones, at 16 kts. and stuck fast. Within hours it became apparent that the worst environmental disaster the world had ever known was slowly unfolding. There were several attempts to pull the tanker off the rocks, but after a crewman was killed in an explosion in the engine room, the vessel was abandoned. On Easter Sunday the *Torrey Canyon* finally broke in two. Oil had been escaping at the rate of 6,000 tons an hour from the ship's 23 full tanks, and Captain Rugiati had deliberately pumped between 30-40,000 tons into the sea during attempts to refloat the ship. A vast oil slick 35 miles (56 km.) long and 15 miles (24 km.) wide soon developed, and much of the coast of Cornwall was fouled. Thousands of seabirds, seals, and other marine life became victims of the tragedy, covered in thick, black, poisonous slime, and it took three

RIGHT: The crippled *Torrey Canyon* oil tanker spills her cargo into the sea in the Seven Stones vicinity of Cornwall, England. The damage to the area's ecology was devastating.

RIGHT: The giant oil tanker, *Torrey Canyon*, trapped on the rocks of Seven Stones. The ship was broken completely in two by the giant seas which pounded her.

ABOVE AND LEFT: The *Torrey Canyon* is a pitiful sight as she breaks up on the rocks. Blame for the disaster rests with the captain of the vessel who was negligent in notoriously perilous waters.

RIGHT: Amidst worsening weather, British warplanes bombed the stricken hulk. Buccaneer fighter-bombers pounded the wreck and aircraft fuel was tipped onto the oil in an attempt to disperse it by burning. Even napalm and high-explosive rockets were used. All efforts were to no avail and the environmental damage was enormous.

BELOW: The Liberian oil tanker *Diane* caught fire after a dawn collision with a German coaster in fog off the Dutch coast on April 4, 1967. Two of her crew of 39 were killed. This photograph shows attempts to quell the flames by tugs which raced to the scene.

years for the fishing industry in the area to begin the process of recovery. Eventually, on March 28, amidst worsening weather, the British government sent warplanes to bomb the stricken hulk. For three days Buccaneer fighter-bombers pounded the wreck, which had split into three. Aircraft fuel was tipped onto the oil in an attempt to get it to burn, and even napalm and high-explosive rockets were used. The pall of smoke could be seen for miles. At the time very little was known about coping with such a disaster. Detergents, which had been used to break up the slick, were later found to be more harmful to marine life than the oil. The board of inquiry, held in Liberia, severely criticized Captain Rugiati and heaped the blame on his shoulders. The board concluded: "Apart from the loss of a fine ship and its cargo, the resulting oil pollution inflicted untold hardship and damage. It was one of the worst disasters in maritime history. The cause was entirely the negligence of the ship's master." Rugiati himself was left a broken man by the experience. He returned home to Genoa suffering from pleurisy and depression and later said: "The worst thing is knowing I could have saved the ship if only I had another 30 seconds to maneuver. I am responsible for what happened and I have been suffering nightmares over it."

Wahine

April 11, 1968
New Zealand

The loss of the *Heraklion* was matched just two years later, in 1968, on the other side of the world by the loss of the *Wahine*, another inter-island passenger and vehicle ferry.

The *Wahine* operated between Wellington on New Zealand's North Island, and Lyttelton on the South Island. She was a busy ship, making the journey between the two ports six times a week and it was her misfortune

LEFT: In the worst disaster in New Zealand's recent history, the inter-island ferry *Wahine* sank just outside Wellington Harbor. The 9,000 ton ship was carrying 604 passengers and a crew of 120 and foundered in relatively shallow waters. Conditions were indescribably bad; winds gusted up to 137 m.p.h. (220 k.p.h.) The photograph shows the *Wahine* as she began to list seriously at about noon. The first lifeboats were leaving but those on the port side were useless and people began to jump into the sea. Within an hour the ship had settled on her side on the bottom.

LEFT: A loaded lifeboat carrying survivors from the *Wahine* crashes ashore in surf. Helpers on the beach rush forward to hold it in place.

to be at sea in the middle of some of the worst recorded weather ever to strike the seas around New Zealand. The *Wahine* was returning to Wellington in the face of gales measuring over 120 m.p.h. (190 k.p.h.) Towering seas contributed to reduce visibility to virtually zero, and the ferry's steering became useless. It was a disastrous loss of control, and the ship drifted toward dangerous rocky shallows. At 06.40 hours on April 11, the *Wahine* struck fast on Barrett's Reef, just outside Wellington harbor. Remarkably the ship was able to free herself, but any sigh of relief was premature. In freeing herself the *Wahine* had holed her hull and lost the starboard propeller. The loss of the propeller was particularly catastrophic as water now began to flood into the engine room. The crew made desperate attempts to get the vessel safely into harbor but the winds worked against them. The ship ran aground for a second time, on this occasion on the eastern entrance to Chaffer's Passage. Water continued to pour into the *Wahine* and the ship began to list dangerously to port. Seeing that little could be done, the order to abandon ship was given at 13.30 hours. Over 700 passengers and crew were on board and made their way to the starboard lifeboats—the only ones that could be launched due to the ship's dangerous list to port. The high winds chose this moment to die down, but the high seas continued, claiming many lives. A headcount revealed that 46 people had died in the incident and five people were also reported as missing.

Seawise University
(formerly *Queen Elizabeth*)

January 9, 1972
Hong Kong

For those sentimental about the triumphs of engineering, the death of the *Queen Elizabeth* was a truly tragic affair. She had been built shortly before World War II, the largest passenger liner ever constructed, and went almost immediately into war service. But in the post war era the ship became a dinosaur.

She was too big for modern ports, too costly to maintain, and there were too few passengers loyal to ocean-going liners in the age of jet airliners. Her last commercial sailing was out of New York on October 30, 1968.

There was an abortive attempt to convert the liner to a tourist attraction in Port Everglades before it was sold to a Hong Kong concern. The 83,673 ton ship was rechristened *Seawise University* but plans to have her converted were scuppered when a fire—possibly started deliberately—swept through the vessel. The blaze was so severe that firefighters finally abandoned their efforts and let it burn out unaided. A day later the *Seawise University* finally rolled over in 43 ft. (13 m.) of water.

ABOVE: March, 1976. The oil
tanker *Olympic Bravery*
breaks up on the rocks.

RIGHT: The end of the *Queen
Elizabeth*. The ship blazes in
Hong Kong Harbor.

Amoco Cadiz

March 16, 1977
Brittany, France

Just 11 years after the world was first alerted to the floating environmental disasters that were waiting to happen, a catastrophic spill which dwarfed the *Torrey Canyon*'s devastated the coastline of northern France. Incredibly, there were many similarities with the *Torrey Canyon*. The *Amoco Cadiz*, built in Spain, was one of the latest and largest supertankers; like the *Torrey Canyon*, she flew the Liberian flag and was crewed by Italians. But at 228,513 tons, she was twice the size of the *Torrey Canyon*, and her cavernous tanks could hold nearly 250,000 tons of crude oil. The unpredictable weather of the English Channel approaches, which had helped to wreck the Spanish Armada in 1588, had once again delivered stormy conditions as the *Amoco Cadiz* made her way toward Rotterdam fully laden with a cargo of crude oil from Iran. Early in the morning of March 16, 1978, her skipper, Captain Bardari, made a slight alteration of course to allow his mighty vessel passage into the "traffic separation scheme," which aims to ensure that vessels do not collide in one of the world's busiest shipping routes. Just after the *Cadiz* had entered the correct northbound lane at 09.45 hours, disaster struck. The ship's steering gear failed completely. Captain Bardari issued a radio warning to all vessels in the area and, luckily, a German salvage tug was in a position to offer assistance. However, before accepting, Captain Bardari was compelled to seek permission from the ship's owners, which meant locating someone in Chicago where it was the middle of the night. It was 15.45 hours before Captain Bardari got through and approval for a tow was given. Six vital hours had been lost. Only then was it discovered that the sheer size and weight of the *Amoco Cadiz* would be too much for one tug to handle. The mighty towing chain snapped like cotton under the tremendous strain of trying to haul the huge ship to safety. As the *Amoco Cadiz* drifted toward the rocky outline of the Brittany coast, the tug tried desperately to secure another line to her stern and Captain Bardari dropped her anchors hoping to secure a drag, but it was all to no avail. She grounded just after 21.00 hours. As the ship was pounded severely by the waves she broke in two and 223,000 tons of oil—four times as much as from the *Torrey Canyon*—spilled out into the sea. Even with improved methods of containing the spill and dealing with slicks, in addition to the lessons learned from before, the environmental effects were still devastating. More than 200 miles (320 km.) of the French coastline was affected, and marine and bird life suffered terribly. The tourist industry of the beautiful Brittany coast was also crippled, and the livelihoods of hundreds of Breton fishermen were ruined.

RIGHT: *Amoco Cadiz* discharges her cargo into the sea off the French coast causing devastation. Extraordinary efforts were made by the people of France to limit the damage, but their efforts made little difference to the huge slick of oil which drifted ashore.

BELOW: The bows of the broken *Amoco Cadiz*.

LEFT, ABOVE AND BELOW: Ten people died when the 27,000 ton *Star Clipper* collided with a road bridge near Gothenburg, Sweden. The bridge connected the islands of Tjorn and Orus. Six cars and two trucks driving over the bridge were plunged into the sea.

RIGHT: January 22, 1980. The Greek cargo ship *Athina* founders off the beach at Brighton, England. The spray gives the impression that she is driving ashore at full steam ahead.

BELOW: Sightseers in London had an unexpected view on April 27, 1980, when the former Clyde paddle steamer, *Old Caledonia*, a floating public house on the Thames, caught fire and was quickly engulfed in smoke and flames. The vessel was built in 1934 at Dunbarton for use as a ferry from Clyde to the Western Isles. During the war she saw duty as an anti-aircraft vessel and as a minesweeper off the coast of Normandy.

Derbyshire

September 10, 1980
China Sea

ABOVE AND LEFT: The ill-fated *Derbyshire* photographed as the *Liverpool Bridge*. The ship had a disturbing tendency to "cry" in heavy weather and it is believed that inherent weakness contributed to her destruction. Investigators suggest that she "snapped like a twig" and was swamped within a minute. The *Derbyshire*'s fate was echoed six years later by her sister ship, *Kowloon Bridge* which also broke in two on the rocks off Ireland.

At almost 1,000 ft. (300 m.) long and 145 ft. (44 m.) wide, the oil-bulk-ore carrier the *Derbyshire* would have dwarfed even the *Titanic*. On September 10, 1980, she was some 200 miles (320 km.) off Japan, heavily laden with iron ore, when she encountered Typhoon Orchid.

The *Derbyshire* was a workhorse, built by Swan Hunter at their Haverton Hill yards on Teeside, England, and initially launched as the *Liverpool Bridge* in 1976. Two days after she was commissioned an auxiliary boiler blew up, killing the third engineer. Nonetheless, she set sail for Hampton Roads in the United States for her first cargo—coal—on July 5, 1976. The last in a six-ship series, she changed her name to the *Derbyshire* in 1977, but continued hauling iron ore, crude oil, and coal to ports around the world.

So it was that the *Derbyshire* found herself in the Pacific, south of Japan, carrying 157,000 tons of iron ore in seven of its nine holds. Typhoon Orchid had surprised meteorologists by "recurving"—turning back on itself—and the 40 ft. (12m.) waves now crashing over the decks of the *Derbyshire* were a shock to the crew. At least, thought Captain Underhill, there was no danger of the heavy iron ore shifting and creating further problems.

Some of the 42 officers and crew, as well as the two wives who were making the trip, were a little more concerned about the giant ship. Some had noticed that it had a tendency to "cry" in heavy seas. Indeed, three men became so disturbed by the ship's terrible screaming that they had insisted on being paid off on an earlier voyage. One, the cook Ronnie Kan, even insisted that the ship "was rotting." He said: "In the galley you were scared to scrub down because so much rust was coming through."

Exactly what happened to cause the *Derbyshire* to founder as she coped with storm-force winds and driving waves will never be known. She sank without trace, unable to even transmit a distress signal. The official inquiry decided simply that the immense ship was overwhelmed by the forces of nature. Relatives of the crewmen, however, believe the ship split in two as it rode one last mighty wave due to a design fault—cracking like a coconut across the deck. As the superstructure began to tilt, a giant wave rolled under the *Derbyshire* and the keel snapped. The next wave would have swamped the ship completely, dragging it down in less than a minute.

A video taken of the wreckage lying 2.5 miles (4 km.) beneath the surface appears to confirm the suspicions of the relatives. There are scores of fragments littering the sea bed when, had the sea claimed it, the carcass would have remained more intact. Marine geologist Chris Davies said:

THIS PAGE: The wreckage of the *Herald of Free Enterprise* which capsized off Zeebrugge, Belgium on March 7, 1987.

BELOW: The ferry is held in place by tugs while rescuers continue to search for victims of the disaster.

"We can discount impact on hitting the seabed because big ships don't just shatter like that, even in violent storms. The spread and the fragmentation of the wreckage in an area known for its lack of deep currents tells us something catastophic must have happened."

One of the *Derbyshire's* sister ships, the *Kowloon Bridge*, broke in two after running aground in Ireland in 1986.

Herald of Free Enterprise

March 6, 1987
Zeebrugge, Belgium

One of the reasons for the sinking of the *Titanic* was that she was considered to be "unsinkable" and the captain consequently failed to act with due caution. Human error again played a role in the dreadful demise of the *Herald of Free Enterprise*; this time the mistake was one of unforgivable stupidity and negligence.

The *Herald of Free Enterprise* was a humble car ferry, with none of the romance and glitz of a trans-Atlantic liner. Most of her 436 passengers, on the evening sailing of March 6, 1987, regarded the four-hour voyage from Zeebrugge in Belgium, across the English Channel to Dover, as no more risky than catching a bus to work. However, they were blissfully unaware that the crew of the 7,951 ton vessel, operated by Townsend Thoresen ferry fleet, had developed a habit of leaving the dockside with the bow doors—through which the cars were loaded—still wide open. Many of the passengers were traveling on special one-day return tickets provided as a travel promotion in one of Britain's mass-circulation daily newspapers. As they settled into their seats and headed for the bars and restaurants on board, Captain David Lewry eased the ship away from Pier Twelve and headed for the harbor entrance. Captain Lewry could not see the bows from the bridge but he knew that a crew member would have been assigned responsibility for operating the doors. As a safety precaution, the chief officer was also expected to double-check that they were shut. Many masters of such vessels were unhappy with this system. For a start, they knew that the design of their ships was inherently unseaworthy. Ocean-going vessels are normally equipped with watertight bulkheads to seal off sections inside the hull. If there is a leak, flooding can often be confined to the area of damage. Roll-on-roll-off car ferries, on the other hand, rely on vast open areas for quick and efficient parking. If water pours in, it is free to slosh around the vehicle decks, instantly destabilizing the ship. The owners had been made aware of the potential problems previously. But when one skipper suggested they should install "doors closed" indicators on the bridge, the reply from head office was: "Do they need an indicator to tell them whether the deck store-

RIGHT: Salvage operations. Showing the scars of her ordeal the *Herald of Free Enterprise* is righted by giant cranes.

RIGHT: The scene of destruction on one of the *Herald*'s car decks.

keeper is awake and sober?" Incredibly, the seaman in charge of the doors that night, Assistant Bosun Mark Stanley, was asleep in his bunk as the *Herald* left Zeebrugge. The officer charged with ensuring that he performed his duty, Chief Officer Leslie Sable, did not check up either. As a result, the doors stayed open. Just 20 minutes into the voyage, as the *Herald* left the shelter of Zeebrugge's three mile (5 km.) long sea wall defense, the waves became large enough to lap over the open doors and into her hull. A night of terror had begun. There was panic on the main passenger decks as the ferry suddenly listed, partially righted herself, and then toppled onto her side like some mortally wounded sea monster. She lay in barely 30 ft. (9 m.), the whole of her starboard clearly visible. In the first 45 seconds of the disaster her hull had half-filled with water. Passenger Andrew Simmons, 30, from Bushey, near London, recalled: "We were trapped for 20 or 30 minutes after the boat went over. Within a minute it went from being upright to on its side, with water gushing in down the stairs and corridors. I and my friend helped a little girl who was only two or three years old, climb up with her father above the water. We were only rescued when people smashed the windows from outside and hauled us out to safety." In those desperate hours, heroes would emerge to perform the most unlikely deeds. Londoner Andrew Parker formed himself into a human bridge by stretching his body across the rising waters. Around 120 people crawled to safety over him and his bravery was later recognized with the George Medal. Almost four in every ten passengers died, a total of 193 victims, and everyone else aboard needed hospital treatment. For dozens of survivors, the legacy of Zeebrugge would be a ceaselessly repeated nightmare. Years later, many continued to seek treatment for post-traumatic stress disorder.

In July 1987, a 29-day inquiry conducted by Mr. Justice Sheen concluded that the ship sunk because neither Mr. Stanley nor Mr. Sable did their jobs properly. Senior master John Kirby was also criticized for his conduct. Ultimate responsibility, said the judge, rested with Captain Lewry. It was, after all, his ship.

Cason

December 5, 1987
Finisterre, Spain

A new peril confronts modern merchant sailors, every bit as dangerous as wreckers or rocks, as the men aboard the *Cason* discovered to their cost.

The freight ship *Cason* ran aground on the Rostro beach near Spain's Cape Finisterre, unleashing its toxic cargo. Tragically, 23 men aboard were suffocated by the fumes, and the nearby towns of Fisterra, Corcubion, and Cee were evacuated when inhabitants developed breathing difficulties.

RIGHT: *Secil Japan*, March 17, 1989. Several meters of water separate the bow and stern of the cargo vessel which ran aground on the well named rocks of Hell's Mouth, North Cornwall, England, during the night.

BELOW: A team of French naval fire brigades speed on their way to the burning 16,000 ton Panamanian-registered oil tanker *Victoria Tuesday* on the Seine river near Rouen, western France, after it collided with the 11,000 ton kerosene loaded Japanese tanker *Fuyo Maru*. The *Victoria* exploded, was cut in two, and later sank. Six persons were missing and two injured in the accident. Officials said that there was no danger of pollution to the river.

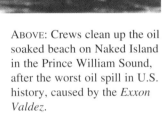

ABOVE: Crews clean up the oil soaked beach on Naked Island in the Prince William Sound, after the worst oil spill in U.S. history, caused by the *Exxon Valdez*.

LEFT: A live guillemot covered in oil from the *Exxon Valdez* tanker in Alaska. An estimated 86,000 birds, 1,000 sea otters, 25,000 fish, 200 seals, and dozens of beavers were all killed. The deadly oil lingered in the coves, destroying thousands of young fish which return each year to spawn in the shallows.

Exxon Valdez

March 1989
Prince William Sound, Alaska, U.S.A.

An environmental catastrophe of enormous magnitude—although the amount of spillage was smaller than that of *Amoco Cadiz* or *Torrey Canyon*—befell the wild and wonderful wilderness of Prince William Sound off Alaska in March 1998.

It should have been a straightforward journey when the 211,469 ton *Exxon Valdez* slipped her moorings just after 21.00 hours on March 23, for the voyage to Long Beach, California. Things were so relaxed that the skipper, Captain Joseph Hazelwood, and a couple of his fellow officers had dropped into the harborside Pipeline Club in Valdez for a few drinks before setting out. Such is the huge Alaskan oil output that captains like Joe Hazelwood spend most of their time on the Valdez-West Coast run. The procedures for entering and exiting port were etched in Hazelwood's memory, and he knew the waters of the Sound like the roads round his home on Long Island, New York. He did not regard the waters as particularly difficult to navigate and anyway, for the next two hours and 20 minutes, harbor pilot William Murphy would have control. Shortly after Murphy had left the ship to return to port on a launch, Hazelwood made two course changes. He was concerned about ice showing on the radar and asked traffic control if he could switch to the clearer inbound sea lane. The controller gave permission, assuring him there were no inbound ships in the vicinity. Hazelwood planned to clear the ice below Busby Island before heading southwest in a narrow passage between the underwater rocks of Bligh Reef and another major ice floe. It was a tricky maneuver, but not one that the captain pondered for too long. In fact, he was so confident that he planned to hand the entire operation over to First Officer Cousins as soon as possible. Cousins had been instructed to make a right-hand turn back into the outbound sea lane after reaching a navigational point near Busby Island. But, unaccountably, he waited six minutes too long before starting the turn and, as a result, the tanker was a mile (1.6 km.) further ahead than she should have been. At six minutes past midnight, Cousins made a desperate phone call to his captain. "I think we are in serious trouble," he said. Hazelwood already knew it. A few seconds earlier he had felt a terrible shuddering, welling up from the bowels of the ship as it ran onto the reef at Prince William Sound. His principal fear as he sprinted to the bridge was that if part of the hull slipped the ship could break her back. A fully laden crude carrier the size of three football pitches would be at the mercy of the waves. As the crisis unfolded, Hazelwood produced a textbook response. By carefully varying his engine power he was able to keep the *Exxon Valdez* tight to the reef, ensuring her

stability. Below water the hull had sustained rents up to 16 ft. (5 m.) long. Eight of the 15 holds had been penetrated, and oil was already in the sea. In the days ahead, ten million gallons would be lost. Only two years earlier a consortium of U.S. oil companies played down the risk of an environmental disaster, stating: "It is highly unlikely that there will ever be a spill of any magnitude." Yet only two months earlier a relatively tiny spill of 1,500 barrels had pushed their fast-reaction clean-up team to its limits. In Prince William Sound that same team was completely out of its league. For a start, it took ten hours to get them to the scene. When they arrived they had no booms—vital equipment if a slick is to be contained—and their detergents proved useless because the sea was too calm. Attempts to burn off the oil proved a waste of time, and the U.S. Coast Guard, required by law to have a vessel on hand for damage-control operations, transparently failed in its duty. Its tiny fleet was cruising 2,000 miles (3,200 km.) away off San Francisco. By Sunday, March 26, the slick covered 900 square miles (1,450 sq. km.). It polluted the hundreds of remote, rocky coves that run the length of Prince William Sound, and once these were fouled there was little hope of solving the problem. An estimated 86,000 birds, 1,000 sea otters, 25,000 fish, 200 seals, and dozens of beavers were all killed. The deadly oil lingered in the coves, destroying thousands of young fish that return each year to spawn in the shallows. America was in uproar at news of the incident, which was portrayed by the media as the worst on record. In fact, the *Exxon Valdez* slick ranks only tenth in the league of oil tanker disasters. It was but a seventh the size of the *Amoco Cadiz* leak, which hit northwest France in March 1977 and only an eighth as big as the world's worst oil tanker spillage caused by the collision of the *Aegean Captain* and the *Atlantic Empress* off Tobago in the Caribbean in 1979.

Marchioness

August 20, 1989
London, Great Britain

Riverboat parties are nothing out of the ordinary. Like many that had gone before, the pleasure craft *Marchioness* was filled with 130 revelers celebrating a 26th birthday when it set off along the Thames in London. But this party was destined to be hideously different to the majority.

Out of the darkness, bearing down on the little river boat, came the 1,180 ton dredger *Bowbelle*. The little cruiser was shattered on impact, while the dredger barely felt a bump. The Thames, picturesque on so many postcards, is riddled with deadly currents and, as the little boat sank, 51 people were swept to their deaths. Those who survived dragged themselves through a murky, panic-stricken nightmare. An inquest later decided that the 51 vic-

RIGHT AND BELOW RIGHT: The wreck of the *Marchioness* is raised from the waters of the Thames.

BELOW: The pleasure cruiser *Marchioness* semi-submerged the day after she collided with *Bowbelle* and sunk. A total of 51 revelers lost their lives.

tims were unlawfully killed, declaring the disaster was caused by "gross negligence." The jury—concerned that there was no lookout posted on the dredger—also called for better training for crews.

Bowbelle herself was doomed. She was sold by her owners to a Portuguese company and renamed *Bom Rei*. While working off Madeira in May 1996 she sank in shallow waters after splitting in two. One crew member was killed.

Neptune

February 17, 1993
Port-au-Prince, Haiti

The loss of life is always potentially huge when catastrophe strikes a ferry. On February 17, 1993, more than 900 passengers drowned when the *Neptune* overturned in a rain squall on the way to Port-au-Prince, Haiti.

The 163 ft. (50 m.) *Neptune* was an old ship, and typical of those used to ferry the impoverished people of Haiti. Its three decks were often a cacophony of peasants, livestock, traders, and others heading for the marketplace 100 miles (160 km.) away. On this particular journey, the ferry was even more overcrowded than usual—nearly 1,500 passengers had swarmed aboard because an earlier ferry had been canceled. Even as it pulled away from port, canoes carried last-minute travelers to join the overloaded boat. About 70 miles (112 km.) into the journey, a small storm caused the rusting hulk to sway. People on the open decks pushed their way into sheltered areas while others panicked as the boat rolled with the swell. A sudden surge of passengers away from the wind-buffeted side caused a catastrophic roll, which saw the *Neptune* capsize, instantly drowning those who had squeezed into the covered decks and sleeping areas. Fewer than 600 were rescued by U.S. Coast Guard helicopters.

Estonia

September 29, 1994
North Sea

In the early hours of September 28, 1994, the loss of the M.S. *Estonia* with a death toll of more than 900 passengers and crew evoked memories of the earlier tragedy at Zeebrugge when the *Herald of Free Enterprise* sank. Like the *Herald*, *Estonia* was a roll-on-roll-off ferry—this one plying its trade across the Baltic Sea from Tallinn to Stockholm. On that fateful trip middle-aged night owls had gathered in the ship's Baltic Bar, listening to the

ABOVE: The *Estonia* rests at port. The bow doors which were blamed for the terrible events can be seen, raised, at the left of the photograph.

RIGHT: A publicity photograph which shows *Estonia*'s Baltic Bar where passengers were listening to music while the storm raged outside.

RIGHT: The rescue team in action at the site of the *Estonia* disaster.

Henry Goy dance band banging out Elvis Presley and Beatles numbers. At least it was better than the sounds of the storm outside. They carried on until well after midnight, when the rolling of the ship in gale-force winds became too much. Besides, most of the 1,049 passengers and crew—mainly businessmen, day trippers, and shoppers—were already tucked up in bed. A few die-hard drinkers made their way to the nearby Pub Admiral for a nightcap. One, oil executive Thomas Grunde, was to be one of only 141 survivors. He said:

"There was a big bang at the front and the ship started to lean a little. Some were afraid, others laughed. Myself, I did not react. Then came another bang, still worse than the first, and the ship started really to lean over. I shot over the dance floor and hit my forehead on a chair or table. A friend helped me to get up, asking how I was feeling. From that moment I had only one thought: I had to get out."

The *Estonia* began shipping water soon after 01.00 hours. But strangely it was not until 01.26 hours that the bridge sent out its first and only distress signal:

"Mayday, Mayday. We have a list of 20 to 30 degrees. Blackout. Mayday."

Why this S.O.S. was not transmitted earlier, and why no attempt was made to muster passengers before the situation became critical, remained two of the key questions for investigators.

So what was the reason for the *Estonia's* catastrophic sinking? All the evidence pointed to a fault in the bow doors, designed to open and close for the loading of vehicles—bow doors similar to those blamed in the *Herald of Free Enterprise* disaster at Zeebrugge. But whereas the error which doomed the *Herald* was down to a sleeping crewman and lax on-board safety systems, it was not immediately obvious why the *Estonia's* doors had failed. One theory was that they had been smashed open by the battering-ram action of the sea. Rune Petterson, an expert in marine hydraulics, carried out work on the *Estonia* in 1988, when she was named the *Sally Viking*. He pointed out that both the bow "visor" and the vehicle ramp—which forms an inner door when raised—were locked in place by the same hydraulic system. "A leak in a cylinder or valve could have made the holding pressure sink, thereby making one or more locks lose their grip on the visor," he said. "The gaskets in the big lifting cylinders have to take the full pressure and then they may have been torn away from their fastenings. The result would be a loosening of the locks on the inner door, allowing the sea to drive into a narrow opening. If this was the case, the force of water entering the ship would be almost incomprehensible. A gap of one square meter, and water entering at a speed of ten meters a second, would mean that in one second ten tons of water would have got in. In the space of a minute,

the ship would have taken on 600 tons." The Estonian government was reluctant to accept this theory, believing it compromised the integrity of the ship and her crew. Johannes Johannson, managing director of the ferry's owners—Estline—pointed out that 40 old mines had been found near the island of Osmussaar, which lay far to the southwest of *Estonia's* last known position. The war of words was of little comfort to the survivors. One, Mr. Heidi Auvinen, 31, recalled:

"I was thrown into the sea and tried to find a place in a lifeboat. I grabbed a rope attached to one of the lifeboats. With great effort and despite waves several meters high I was able to drag myself aboard. The raging sea looked terrible, with corpses floating in the water, lifeboats, abandoned clothing. I heard distant cries for help, groaning. The memory will haunt me forever."

Andrus Maidre, a 19-year-old Estonian, witnessed the most heartbreaking sight of all. "Some old people had already given up hope and were just sitting there crying," he said. "I also stepped over children who were wailing and holding onto the railing."

Among the first ships to answer the Mayday was the ferry *Isabella*. One of its passengers, Swede Mr. Hemming Eriksson, painted a dreadful picture of the carnage that confronted him. "There were hundreds of bodies that were bobbing up and down in the sea," he said. "Many were dressed only in underwear and life vests. Some of them moved, so you could see they were living, but we had no chance to bring them up in the heavy sea. The worst was when the bodies got sucked into the propellers."

Achille Lauro

November 30, 1994
Indian Ocean

Few ships have known the notoriety of the *Achille Lauro*, a luxury liner that came into service in 1947. This 23,629 ton ship was targeted by Palestinian terrorists in October 1985, who then held passengers hostage. The world recoiled in horror when they killed wheelchair-bound passenger Leon Klinghoffer by throwing him overboard.

Terrorism aside, the *Achille Lauro* also rammed the boat of an Italian fisherman in 1971, causing his death. A decade later two more people died trying escape an on-board fire. The end came when a fire thought to have been caused by a burst piston head in the engine room swept through the ship when she was about 120 miles (190 km.) off the East African coast of Somalia during a cruise from Genoa to Durban. Four people died in the drama, although 1,000 passengers and crew escaped to safety.

LEFT: The ill-fated *Achille Lauro* lists to starboard as lifecraft escape. This unfortunate ship was the scene of several tragedies before she finally caught fire off the east coast of Africa.

BELOW: The Italian cruise ship *Achille Lauro* burns some 100 miles off the Somalia coast. Over 1,000 passengers and crew were rescued and transported to several ports in the region.

Sea Empress

February 15, 1996
Milford Haven, Great Britain

BELOW: The 147,000 ton *Sea Empress* on the rocks outside the British port of Milford Haven. The oil spill decimated wildlife as well as ruining the tourist trade of the region.

"There was a shuddering vibration, then a sound from the deck below of liquid being forced under pressure and a strong smell of oil." That's how accident investigators described what happened when the 147,000 ton Liberian-registered tanker *Sea Empress* ran onto rocks while entering Milford Haven docks. In three days an estimated 72,000 tons of crude oil escaped from the ruptured tanks, causing havoc for local sea-going wildlife along 120 miles (190 km.) of Britain's west coast, and decimating the tourist trade. Fishing was banned in the area after the disaster as a precaution for public safety. Pilot error and insufficient tugs for the maneuver into the harbor were blamed.